Sunset
Homemade Soups

By the Editors
of Sunset Books
and
Sunset Magazine

Lane Publishing Co.
Menlo Park, California

RESEARCH & TEXT
CLAIRE COLEMAN
MARY JANE SWANSON

COORDINATING EDITOR
CORNELIA FOGLE

SPECIAL CONSULTANT
JOAN GRIFFITHS

DESIGN
CYNTHIA HANSON

ILLUSTRATIONS
SUSAN JAEKEL

PHOTO STYLIST
JOANN MASAOKA

A mellow blending of flavors

—that's what characterizes home-made soup. Hot or cold, chunky or smooth, sweet or savory, soups offer an astonishing array of choices. Moreover, they're among the most versatile of all foods. Soups can be hearty enough to be the entrée at lunch or dinner, or light enough for sipping before a holiday feast. Best of all, most soups are prepared from familiar ingredients and are easy to make, often well ahead of when you need to serve them.

Our collection of recipes begins with the basics—simple, flavorful stocks which can become the starting point for many of the other soups in the book. In the following chapters, you'll find clear broths and velvety smooth purées to whet the appetite, simple yet substantial soups to offer with a sandwich or salad, hearty meal-in-a-bowl entrées brimming with chunks of meat and vegetables, and sweet soups suitable for dessert or brunch.

In our features we offer hints for serving, storing, and reheating soups; for making seasoned croutons and other garnishes; for cooking soup in a microwave oven; and for baking breads that can accompany soup courses. Finally, we present ideas for menus that feature soups.

Special thanks to Fran Feldman and Rebecca LaBrum for editing the manuscript. We also thank Animal Crackers, The Best of All Worlds, Brown's China & Glass, Cooks' Junction, Domus, Rorke's, Taylor & Ng, William Ober Co., and Williams-Sonoma for their generosity in sharing props for use in our photographs.

Cover:

Almost a meal in itself, hearty Beef & Bean Minestrone (page 63) features a beef-enriched broth enhanced by shell-shaped pasta and an abundance of vegetables—potatoes, zucchini, leeks, kidney and green beans, tomatoes, and peas. Pair this colorful Italian favorite with crunchy bread sticks for a satisfying supper. Cover design by Williams and Ziller Design. Photo styling by JoAnn Masaoka. Food styling by Cynthia Scheer. Photography by Nikolay Zurek.

Photographers:

Victor Budnik: page 75. **Glenn Christiansen:** page 31. **Michael Lamotte:** page 23. **Norman A. Plate:** page 42. **Tom Wyatt:** page 47. **Nikolay Zurek:** pages 18, 26, 34, 39, 67, 70, 78, 83, 86, 91, 94.

Editor, Sunset Books: David E. Clark
First printing September 1985

CONTENTS

FLAVORFUL HOMEMADE STOCKS

STARTING POINTS FOR

THE MOST DELICIOUS

HOMEMADE SOUPS

The basis of a truly homemade soup is a homemade stock. Meat and fish stocks are made by slowly simmering the bones and trimmings of meat or fish with vegetables and seasonings; vegetable stocks use only fresh vegetables and seasonings for their base.

Though canned broth, bouillon cubes, and stock base are convenient alternatives, it's easy to make your own stock—and its rich flavor is a just reward.

In this chapter are recipes for the chicken, beef, fish, and Chinese stocks called for in our recipes. Also included are two vegetable stocks that can substitute for the above in many cases.

CHICKEN STOCK

It's easy to accumulate enough chicken bones for stock, especially if you're in the habit of cutting up chickens at home. Just save the wings, backs, and necks, and even the breastbones and skins from boned chicken breasts; store them in the freezer until you have about 5 pounds.

  5 pounds bony chicken pieces (such as necks, backs, and wings)
12 cups water
  2 carrots, cut into chunks
  2 medium-size onions, quartered
  2 stalks celery, cut into pieces (include leaves, if any)
  1 bay leaf
  6 whole black peppercorns
  ¼ teaspoon thyme leaves
  2 sprigs parsley

In a 6 to 8-quart pan, combine chicken pieces, water, carrots, onions, celery, bay leaf, peppercorns, thyme, and parsley. Bring to a boil over high heat; reduce heat, cover, and simmer for 2½ to 3 hours. Let cool.

Pour stock through a wire strainer and discard vegetables, bones, and seasonings. Cover and refrigerate for up to 4 days; lift off and discard fat before using or freezing. To freeze, transfer stock to freezer containers, leaving about an inch for expansion at top. Cover and freeze for up to 6 months. Makes about 12 cups.

CHINESE CHICKEN OR PORK STOCK

Seasoned with ginger and green onions, this stock makes a good starting point for Chinese soups. You can make it from chicken or pork bones, or both.

  3 pounds bony chicken pieces (such as necks, backs, and wings), uncooked pork bones and trimmings, or a combination of both
  8 cups water
  2 quarter-size slices fresh ginger, crushed
  2 green onions (including tops), halved crosswise

In a 5 to 6-quart pan, combine chicken pieces, water, ginger, and onions. Bring to a boil over high heat; skim off any foam from the surface. Reduce heat, cover, and simmer for 2 hours. Let cool.

Pour stock through a wire strainer and discard bones and seasonings. Cover and refrigerate for up to 4 days; lift off and discard fat before using or freezing. To freeze, transfer stock to freezer containers, leaving about an inch for expansion at top. Cover and freeze for up to 6 months. Makes about 6 cups.

BEEF STOCK

All you need to make beef stock are lots of bones, a few vegetables, and some herbs and spices. As the stock simmers, it gives your kitchen a wonderful aroma; later, when you use it for cooking, its rich flavor will permeate your soups.

  4 pounds beef and veal shanks (or all beef shanks), cut up
12 cups water
  2 carrots, cut into chunks
  2 medium-size onions, quartered
  2 stalks celery, cut into pieces (include leaves, if any)
  1 bay leaf
  2 whole cloves garlic
  2 whole cloves
  6 whole black peppercorns
  ¼ teaspoon thyme leaves

Place shanks in a roasting pan and bake, uncovered, in a 450° oven until browned (20 to 25 minutes). Transfer to a 6 to 8-quart pan. Add 1 cup of the water to roasting pan and stir to scrape up browned bits; then pour over shanks along with remaining 11 cups water. Add carrots, onions, celery, bay leaf, garlic, cloves, peppercorns, and thyme.

Bring to a boil over high heat; reduce heat, cover, and simmer until meat falls from bones (about 2½ hours). Let cool.

Pour stock through a wire strainer and discard meat, bones, vegetables, and seasonings. Cover and refrigerate for up to 4 days; lift off and discard fat before using or freezing. To freeze, transfer stock to freezer containers, leaving about an inch for expansion at top. Cover and freeze for up to 6 months. Makes about 12 cups.

ALL-PURPOSE MEAT STOCK

Follow directions for **Beef Stock,** but instead of using only beef or veal shanks, use any combination of the following: **lamb necks; ham hocks;** and **veal, beef, pork, or lamb shanks.**

FISH STOCK

Any seafood soup is enhanced when it's made with a well-seasoned fish stock. And you'll find that fish stock is faster to make than other stocks. If you aren't in the habit of saving fish bones, heads, and trimmings, ask for them at a fish market.

    2 tablespoons butter or margarine
    1 cup *each* finely chopped onions and
        chopped parsley
    4 pounds fish bones, trimmings, and heads
        (preferably those of lean, mild-flavored,
        white-fleshed fish)
    3 tablespoons lemon juice
 1½ cups dry white wine
    8 cups water

In a 6 to 8-quart pan, melt butter over medium-high heat. Add onions and parsley and cook, stirring occasionally, just until onion is soft (about 5 minutes). Reduce heat to low. Place fish bones, trimmings, and heads over vegetables; add lemon juice and cook, shaking pan occasionally, for 5 minutes. Add wine and simmer, uncovered, until liquid is reduced by half (20 to 30 minutes).

Add water; bring to a boil over high heat and boil rapidly, uncovered, until liquid is reduced by half (about 30 minutes). Let cool.

Pour stock through a wire strainer and discard vegetables and fish bones, trimmings, and heads. Cover and refrigerate for up to 2 days. To freeze, transfer stock to freezer containers, leaving about an inch for expansion at top. Cover and freeze for up to 6 months. Makes about 4 cups.

ROOT VEGETABLE STOCK

Vegetable stocks appeal to those who love good soup but don't wish to use a meat-based broth.

    2 tablespoons butter or margarine
    3 large carrots, coarsely chopped
    1 large turnip, coarsely chopped
    2 large stalks celery, thinly sliced (include
        leaves, if any)
    2 large onions, chopped
   12 cups water
    6 large parsley sprigs
   ½ bay leaf
    1 teaspoon thyme leaves
    2 cloves garlic
   10 whole black peppercorns

In a 6 to 8-quart pan, melt butter over medium-high heat. Add carrots, turnip, celery, and onions. Cook, stirring occasionally, until onions are golden (about 15 minutes).

Stir in water, parsley, bay leaf, thyme, garlic, and peppercorns. Bring to a boil over high heat; reduce heat, cover, and simmer for 1½ hours. Let cool.

Pour stock through a wire strainer and discard vegetables and seasonings. Cover and refrigerate for up to 4 days. To freeze, transfer stock to freezer containers, leaving about an inch for expansion at top. Cover and freeze for up to 6 months. Makes about 10 cups.

GREEN VEGETABLE STOCK

Like chicken and beef stocks, vegetable stocks can be made from purchased instant stock base—but the homemade version offers a better-tasting and more wholesome alternative.

This stock is flavored with greens of the season and is best made with two different varieties (4 cups of each). Choose from spinach, Swiss chard, kale, and mustard greens; the latter two make a stronger-flavored stock.

    8 cups coarsely shredded, lightly packed
        greens (see suggestions above)
    1 small head green cabbage, coarsely
        shredded
    1 cup lightly packed parsley sprigs
    2 large stalks celery, chopped (include
        leaves, if any)
    1 large onion, coarsely chopped, or 2
        medium-size leeks, sliced (include lower
        third of green tops)
    3 large cloves garlic, minced or pressed
    1 teaspoon thyme leaves
    1 bay leaf
   15 whole black peppercorns
   12 cups water

In a 6 to 8-quart enamel or stainless steel pan, combine greens, cabbage, parsley, celery, onion, garlic, thyme, bay leaf, peppercorns, and water. Bring to a boil over high heat; reduce heat and simmer, uncovered, for 1½ hours. Let cool.

Pour stock through a wire strainer and discard vegetables and seasonings. Cover and refrigerate for up to 4 days. To freeze, transfer stock to freezer containers, leaving about an inch for expansion at top. Cover and freeze for up to 6 months. Makes about 8 cups.

HINTS FOR THE SOUP CHEF

Making soup is a forgiving art—most soups readily tolerate additions, deletions, or other minor changes, allowing the cook great flexibility. This flexibility extends to the way you serve soup; presentation possibilities are limited only by your imagination. And—perhaps most useful of all—most soups take well to both short and long-term storage, even improving in flavor as they stand.

Here are some guidelines for serving, storing, and reheating soup.

Serving ideas. Though the classic soup server is a lidded tureen, any handsome pot, bowl, or casserole will do if the size is appropriate. For a smooth, pourable soup, a pitcher is a handy dispenser.

For individual servings, consider offering a hot soup in a cup or mug, or a chilled one in a pretty glass. Keep in mind that deep bowls are best for soups that cool quickly; wide, shallow containers suit thick soups. Be sure to use overproof bowls for any soups with a broiled or baked topping.

To maintain a soup's temperature over a period of time, use icers (cups nestled in bowls filled with ice), an insulated jug or vacuum bottle, an electric warming tray, candle warmers, or an alcohol burner.

Soup storage. Because the flavor of many soups (especially the hearty ones) improves with age, it's fine to make them ahead of time or serve them as leftovers.

As a rule of thumb, almost all soups can be stored in the refrigerator for 4 to 5 days, except those made with fish or shellfish. These should be kept for only 1 to 2 days.

You can even freeze most soups for up to 6 months. But before you freeze any soup, be aware of a few do's and don'ts. Since potatoes may get mealy, omit them from soups you plan to freeze. Instead, cook potatoes in the soup when you're reheating it or add freshly cooked potatoes just before serving.

Let the soup cool completely before freezing. Skim and discard any fat; then pour the soup into freezer containers. Liquids expand upon freezing, so leave about an inch of space beneath the container lids.

Homemade stock freezes very successfully, too, making it an even more appealing alternative to canned broth or instant bouillon. Store it in containers as directed above; or freeze it in ice cube trays, then release the cubes and store them in freezer bags, ready to use whenever you need a small amount of broth.

Reheating tips. You don't have to worry about alterations in flavor when reheating soups, but you can expect some minor changes in texture and appearance. Dense soups tend to thicken upon storing; dilute them with a little stock, water, cream, or milk while reheating to thin them to the desired consistency. If the soup contains green vegetables, they may lose some of their bright color; shellfish may toughen upon reheating.

Reheat soups straight from the refrigerator (let frozen soups thaw in the refrigerator overnight). Cook over medium heat, stirring occasionally, until the soup is heated through. Thick purées and soups containing milk, cream, eggs, or cheese require a little extra care; heat them very slowly, stirring often, just until steaming. Be sure not to let them boil or their ingredients may separate.

FIRST-COURSE
S^{OUP}S

SIMPLE BROTHS,

CREAMS & PURÉES

TO BEGIN A MEAL

Whether the occasion is a festive dinner party or an informal family supper, soups never fail to make an appealing first course. Our recipes offer a variety of choices—from hot soups to icy cold ones, from clear broths to creamy vegetable purées. All are ideal, light meal-openers.

You'll enjoy experimenting with different containers—cups, mugs, small bowls, even vegetable shells. Because the soups are smooth, they take well to creative garnishing, also.

When estimating quantities, keep in mind that we consider a serving of a first-course soup to be about one cup.

• ORANGE-BEEF BROTH •

The aroma of oranges is subtle but appealing in this simple beef broth. It's perfect for sipping before a holiday feast.

> 2 large navel oranges
> 3 tablespoons butter or margarine
> 2 cans (10½ oz. *each*) condensed beef broth
> 1 soup can water
> ½ cup orange juice
> 1 teaspoon sugar
> 2 whole cloves

With a vegetable peeler, cut 4 thin strips (each about an inch long) of orange peel (colored part only); set aside for garnish.

Holding fruit over a 2 to 3-quart pan to catch juices, cut all remaining peel, including white membrane, from oranges; cut segments free and place in pan along with butter. Cook over medium-low heat for 3 minutes.

Add broth, water, orange juice, sugar, and cloves. Bring to a boil over high heat; reduce heat, cover, and simmer for 10 minutes. Press broth mixture through a wire strainer; discard oranges and cloves. Pour broth into cups, mugs, or small soup bowls; garnish each serving with a twist of reserved orange peel. Makes 4 servings.

• WINE CONSOMMÉ •

A Zinfandel or Cabernet Sauvignon would be an excellent choice for making this classic beef consommé accented with wine.

> 4 cups Beef Stock (page 5) or regular-
>   strength canned beef broth
> 1 egg white, lightly beaten
> 1 cup dry red wine
> 1 teaspoon sugar
>   Dash of lemon juice
>   Salt and pepper
>   Thin lemon slices

Line a wire strainer with a moistened muslin cloth or several layers of moistened cheesecloth.

In a 2 to 3-quart pan, bring stock to a boil over high heat. To clarify, stir in egg white and bring to a full boil; pour through lined strainer, discard egg white, and return clarified liquid to pan. Return to a boil and add wine, sugar, and lemon juice. Season to taste with salt and pepper. Garnish individual servings with lemon slices. Makes about 4 servings.

JELLIED WINE CONSOMMÉ

Soften 2 envelopes **unflavored gelatin** in ½ cup cold **water.** Prepare **Wine Consommé**, adding gelatin mixture to boiling clarified broth along with wine, sugar, and lemon juice. Stir until gelatin is dissolved. Refrigerate until set; whip with a wire whisk or a fork. Serve with **lemon wedges.**

• FRESH MUSHROOM BEEF BROTH •

For a light first course with delightful flavor, try this quick and easy broth enlivened with mushrooms.

> 2 tablespoons butter or margarine
> 1 small onion, chopped
> ½ teaspoon curry powder
> ½ pound mushrooms, sliced
> 1 small clove garlic, minced or pressed
> 3½ cups Beef Stock (page 5) or regular-
>   strength canned beef broth
> 1 tablespoon lemon juice
> 1 teaspoon Worcestershire
> ¼ teaspoon dry basil
> 1 green onion (including top), thinly sliced

In a 3-quart pan, melt butter over medium heat. Add chopped onion and curry powder and cook, stirring occasionally, until onion is soft (about 10 minutes). Add mushrooms and garlic and cook, stirring occasionally, until most of the mushroom liquid has evaporated (about 5 minutes).

Add stock, lemon juice, Worcestershire, and basil. Bring to a boil and boil for 1 minute. Top each serving with green onion. Makes 4 servings.

• LEMON CONSOMMÉ •

Very easy to make, this lemon-scented consommé is especially good preceding a delicate fish entrée.

> 3 cups Chicken Stock (page 5) or regular-
>   strength canned chicken broth
> ½ teaspoon grated lemon peel
> 2 tablespoons lemon juice
>   Thin lemon slices

In a 1½ to 2-quart pan, bring stock to a boil over high heat. Stir in lemon peel and lemon juice. Garnish individual servings with lemon slices. Makes 3 or 4 servings.

• CHILE-LEMON BROTH •

This piquant broth is elegant in its simplicity. Fresh ginger, garlic, lemon, and hot red chile give it an Oriental flavor; tiny shrimp, fresh coriander, and lemon slices further enhance the flavor while providing visual interest.

   3 **cups Chicken Stock (page 5) or regular-strength canned chicken broth**
   1 **small dried hot red chile**
   1 **strip lemon peel (about 3 inches long), yellow part only**
   1 **thin slice (1 by 3 inches) fresh ginger**
   1 **clove garlic, minced or pressed**
  ¼ **pound small cooked shrimp**
   1 **tablespoon lemon juice**
     Fresh cilantro (coriander) sprigs
     Thin lemon slices

In a 1½ to 2-quart pan, combine stock, chile, lemon peel, ginger, and garlic. Bring to a boil over high heat; reduce heat, cover, and simmer for 20 minutes. Strain if desired. Add shrimp and heat for about 1 minute; stir in lemon juice. Garnish individual servings with cilantro sprigs and lemon slices. Makes 4 servings.

• SPANISH GARLIC SOUP •

Hot chicken broth, buttery toast cubes, eggs, and garlic are the focal flavors of this savory Spanish soup. In its native land, it's known as *sopa de ajo*.

   4 **slices firm-textured white bread, crusts removed**
   2 **tablespoons butter or margarine**
   3 **cloves garlic, minced or pressed**
 3½ **cups Chicken Stock (page 5) or regular-strength canned chicken broth**
   1 **bay leaf**
   1 **teaspoon lemon juice**
   4 **eggs**
     Finely chopped parsley or coarsely chopped fresh cilantro (coriander)

Cut bread into ½-inch cubes. In a wide frying pan, melt butter over medium heat; add garlic and bread cubes and cook, stirring often, until bread is lightly browned. Remove from pan and set aside. Pour stock into pan; add bay leaf and lemon juice. Bring to a simmer over medium heat. Break eggs, one at a time, into a saucer; carefully slip each into hot broth and cook until whites are set but yolks are still runny (3 to 4 minutes).

Transfer eggs to 4 individual soup bowls; ladle broth over eggs and sprinkle each serving with bread cubes and parsley. Makes 4 servings.

• EGG DROP SOUP •

Long, delicate strands of egg distinguish this classic Chinese first course; they're formed when you stir beaten eggs into hot chicken broth.

   1 **large bunch watercress or 2 cups coarsely sliced spinach leaves**
   4 **cups Chinese Chicken or Pork Stock (page 5), Chicken Stock (page 5), or regular-strength canned chicken broth**
   2 **teaspoons *each* dry sherry and soy sauce**
   2 **eggs**
     Salt

Wash watercress and discard thick stems; break long sprigs in half. In a 2-quart pan, bring stock, sherry, and soy to a boil over high heat. Add watercress; reduce heat and simmer, uncovered, for 2 minutes.

Meanwhile, beat eggs lightly. Remove pan from heat. Slowly add eggs to soup, stirring constantly, until they form long threads. Season to taste with salt. Makes about 4 servings.

• NOODLE & PEA BROTH •

Sweet and crunchy sugar snap peas, with their edible pods, star in this unusual soup. Served in small bowls, it's an ideal springtime meal-opener.

  ¼ **pound sugar snap peas, ends and strings removed**
   6 **cups Chicken Stock (page 5) or regular-strength canned chicken broth**
   2 **whole star anise (or ¼ teaspoon crushed anise seeds and 2 cinnamon sticks, *each* 2 inches long)**
  ¾ **teaspoon grated fresh ginger**
   1 **ounce thin dry pasta strands, such as capellini or vermicelli**

Slice each pea diagonally into ¼ to ½-inch-wide pieces; set aside.

In a 4 to 5-quart pan, combine stock, star anise, and ginger. Bring to a boil over high heat. Add pasta; return to a boil and cook, uncovered, until pasta is tender (about 3 minutes). Remove star anise. Add sliced peas; return to a boil, then serve immediately. Makes about 6 servings.

AVGOLEMONO

Avgo (eggs) and *lemono* (lemon juice) are the basis of this light and luscious Greek specialty. When adding the egg mixture, be sure to use low heat so the eggs don't curdle.

> 4 **cups Chicken Stock (page 5) or regular-strength canned chicken broth**
> 4 **eggs**
> ¼ **cup lemon juice**
>   **Lemon slices**

In a 3-quart pan, bring stock to a boil over medium heat. Meanwhile, in a large bowl, beat eggs until light and foamy; then beat in lemon juice. Slowly pour about 1 cup of the hot stock into egg mixture, beating constantly. Reduce heat to low. Slowly pour egg mixture into pan, beating constantly. Cook, stirring, until soup thickens. Garnish individual servings with lemon slices. Makes about 4 servings.

AVOCADO MADRILÈNE

Pictured on page 18

A consommé madrilène is a broth flavored with tomato and served hot, cold, or jellied; the word *madrilène* is French and means "of Madrid." The broth in this version is jellied and then diced into cubes, producing a cool, shimmering first course.

> 2 **cans (10½ oz. *each*) condensed beef consommé**
> 3 **cups tomato juice**
> ½ **green bell pepper, seeded and chopped**
> 1 **small onion, sliced**
> 2 **teaspoons *each* chili powder and sugar**
> 2 **whole cloves**
> ½ **teaspoon oregano leaves**
> ¼ **teaspoon salt**
> 2 **envelopes unflavored gelatin**
> 2 **ripe avocados**
>   **Sour cream**
>   **Chopped chives or green onion (optional)**

In a 3-quart pan, combine consommé with 2½ cups of the tomato juice. Add bell pepper, onion, chili powder, sugar, cloves, oregano, and salt. Bring to a boil over medium-high heat; reduce heat, cover, and simmer for 20 minutes. Pour mixture through a wire strainer, pressing to release juice from vegetables; discard vegetables and cloves.

Meanwhile, soften gelatin in remaining ½ cup tomato juice. Add to strained liquid and heat, stir-ring, until gelatin is dissolved. Pour into a shallow baking pan and refrigerate until set.

Cut jellied madrilène into ½ to ¾-inch cubes in pan; remove with a spatula and pile into individual bowls. Pit, peel, and dice avocados; distribute over madrilène, then top with sour cream. Garnish with chives, if desired. Makes 6 to 8 servings.

JAPANESE MISO SOUP

In Japan, protein-rich soybeans are used to produce a variety of foods, among them tofu (bean curd), soy sauce, and miso. Miso, a fermented soybean paste, contributes a distinctive maltlike flavor to many Japanese dishes, such as this clear soup.

To prepare the following recipes, buy white miso; it's milder in flavor and less salty than red miso. We've suggested green onions and cubes of tofu as embellishments, but you can substitute others such as a watercress sprig, a few thin carrot or mushroom slices, or small spinach leaves.

> 5 **cups dashi (basic soup stock—directions follow)**
> ¼ **cup white miso (fermented soybean paste)**
> ¼ **pound medium-firm (regular) tofu (bean curd), drained and cut into ½-inch cubes**
> 1 **green onion (including top), cut into 1-inch-long julienne strips**

In a 2 to 3-quart pan, combine dashi, miso, and tofu. Bring to a boil over high heat. Garnish individual servings with onion. Makes 6 servings.

Dashi. Dashi is made from dried bonito flakes (*katsuobushi*) and dried tangle seaweed (*kombu*). A convenient alternative is *dashi-no-moto*, instant dashi that's available in several forms. Prepare it according to package directions. Regular-strength chicken broth (skimmed of fat) is also an accept-able substitute for dashi, though the flavor isn't authentic.

MISO SOUP WITH EGG

In a 2 to 3-quart pan, combine 4 cups **dashi** and ¼ cup **white miso.** Bring to a boil over high heat. Meanwhile, lightly beat 1 **egg.** Swirling soup in pan, add egg very slowly, letting it trickle into pan (cooked egg will form thin, ribbonlike strands). Remove from heat. If desired, add 2 teaspoons **mirin** (sweet rice wine) or cream sherry.

Place a twist of **orange peel** or lemon peel in each of 4 to 6 small soup bowls; ladle in soup. Sprinkle with slices of **green onion** (including top). Makes 4 to 6 servings.

• CHESTNUT SOUP •

If you've ever prepared fresh chestnuts, you'll certainly appreciate the convenience of buying canned chestnut purée. Imported from France, the purée is available in the gourmet section of many markets.

      1 tablespoon olive oil or salad oil
      1 cup sliced celery
    ⅔ cup sliced carrots
    1½ cups chopped onions
    3½ cups Chicken Stock (page 5) or regular-
         strength canned chicken broth
    ¼ cup chopped parsley
    ¼ cup port
      3 whole cloves
      1 can (15½ oz.) chestnut purée
    ½ cup half-and-half (light cream)
         Salt and pepper
         Chopped chives

Heat oil in a 3 to 4-quart pan over medium heat; add celery, carrots, and onions and cook, stirring occasionally, until onions are soft (about 10 minutes). Stir in stock, parsley, port, and cloves. Cover and simmer until vegetables are very tender (about 30 minutes).

Discard cloves, then stir in chestnut purée and remove from heat. Whirl chestnut mixture, a portion at a time, in a food processor or blender until smooth. Return to pan, stir in half-and-half, and season to taste with salt and pepper. Heat until steaming. Garnish with chives. Makes 8 servings.

SHIITAKE SPINACH SOUP

Long ago, shiitake were called "the elixir of life" by Orientals who believed that the mushroom helped keep them young and vigorous; shiitake are still valued today for their rich, meaty flavor and velvety succulence. In this soup, they give substance to a light beef broth with spinach and potato.

      8 to 12 medium-size fresh or 1 ounce dried
         shiitake mushrooms
      2 tablespoons butter or margarine
      1 small onion, finely chopped
    5½ cups Beef Stock (page 5) or regular-
         strength canned beef broth
      1 medium-size thin-skinned potato, peeled
         and cut into ½-inch cubes
    1½ cups firmly packed spinach leaves
         Finely chopped parsley (optional)

If using dried mushrooms, soak in warm water to cover for 30 minutes; drain. For fresh *or* dried mushrooms, cut off and discard stems; cut caps into ⅛-inch-wide slivers.

In a 4 to 5-quart pan, melt butter over medium heat. Add onion and cook, stirring often, until soft (about 10 minutes). Add stock and mushrooms. Cover and bring to a boil over high heat. Add potato; reduce heat, cover, and simmer until potato is fork-tender (about 10 minutes).

Cut large spinach leaves into strips. Add spinach to stock mixture and cook, uncovered, until just wilted (1 to 2 minutes). Sprinkle individual servings with parsley, if desired. Makes about 6 servings.

• CREAM OF PISTACHIO SOUP •

Pistachios, used both as an ingredient and as a crunchy garnish, add mellow flavor to this hot soup. Whole chives dress up its appearance.

    1½ cups shelled (3 cups or ¾ lb. in shell) raw,
         roasted, or roasted salted pistachios
    ¼ cup butter or margarine
      1 small onion, finely chopped
    ½ cup chopped celery
      1 clove garlic, minced or pressed
      2 tablespoons dry sherry
      6 cups Chicken Stock (page 5) or regular-
         strength canned chicken broth
    ¼ cup long-grain white rice
      2 parsley sprigs
      1 small bay leaf
      1 cup whipping cream
         Whole chives

Rub pistachios in a clean dishtowel to remove as much of skins as possible; then set aside.

In a 4 to 5-quart pan, melt butter over medium heat. Add onion, celery, and garlic and cook, stirring often, until onion is very soft but not browned (about 15 minutes). Add sherry, stock, rice, parsley, bay leaf, and ¾ cup of the pistachios. Bring to a boil over high heat; reduce heat, cover, and simmer until rice is tender (about 25 minutes). Discard bay leaf.

Whirl pistachio mixture, a portion at a time, in a food processor or blender until very smooth; pour through a wire strainer and discard residue. Return to pan. Stir in cream and heat until steaming.

Garnish individual servings with chives and sprinkle with remaining ¾ cup pistachios. Makes 6 to 8 servings.

YOGURT ALMOND BISQUE

Hot soups that can be sipped from cups or mugs are always welcome at cool-weather picnics, and this tangy yogurt soup thickened with ground almonds is no exception. You can keep it warm in a pre-heated vacuum bottle for up to 3 hours.

    3 tablespoons butter or margarine
    1 small onion, finely chopped
    1 teaspoon paprika
    ⅛ teaspoon *each* ground cloves and ground mace
    ¼ teaspoon *each* thyme leaves and ground cumin
    4 cups Chicken Stock (page 5) or regular-strength canned chicken broth
    1 cup blanched almonds
    1 cup plain yogurt
    1 tablespoon all-purpose flour
    ¼ cup dry vermouth
      Salt and ground red pepper (cayenne)

In a 2 to 3-quart pan, melt butter over medium heat. Add onion and cook, stirring occasionally, until soft (about 10 minutes). Stir in paprika, cloves, mace, thyme, cumin, and stock.

Whirl almonds in a food processor or blender until finely ground. Add to soup. Bring to a boil over high heat; reduce heat, cover, and simmer for 30 minutes.

Stir together yogurt and flour; with a wire whisk, stir into soup. Bring to a boil over medium-high heat, stirring constantly; add vermouth. Season to taste with salt and red pepper. Makes 6 servings.

MARITATA SOUP

Maritata means "married" in Italian, and maritata soup is certainly a happy marriage of flavors. Sweet butter, Parmesan cheese, egg yolks, and thick cream combine to create a rich and velvety broth.

    5½ cups Chicken Stock (page 5) or regular-strength canned chicken broth
      2 ounces vermicelli
    ½ cup (¼ lb.) unsalted butter, softened
      1 cup (3 to 5 oz.) freshly grated Parmesan cheese
      4 egg yolks
      1 cup whipping cream
        Ground nutmeg (optional)

In a 4 to 5-quart pan, bring stock to a boil over high heat. Break vermicelli into short lengths and add to pan. Reduce heat to medium and simmer until pasta is tender (3 to 5 minutes).

Meanwhile, in a bowl, beat butter, cheese, and egg yolks until well blended; gradually beat in cream. Slowly pour about 1 cup of the hot stock into egg mixture, beating constantly.

Reduce heat to low. Slowly pour egg mixture into pan, beating constantly. Dust individual servings with nutmeg, if desired. Makes about 6 servings.

CREAMY HERBED WALNUT SOUP

Walnuts add body and flavor to this savory soup seasoned with sherry and herbs.

    1½ cups chopped walnuts
      2 cups milk
    ½ bay leaf
    ¼ teaspoon *each* thyme leaves and dry basil
      2 tablespoons chopped parsley
      2 tablespoons butter or margarine
      1 medium-size onion, thinly sliced
    ½ cup thinly sliced celery
      2 tablespoons all-purpose flour
      3 cups Chicken Stock (page 5) or regular-strength canned chicken broth
      2 tablespoons dry sherry
        Salt and pepper
        Finely chopped chives or green onion, including tops (optional)

Place walnuts in a pan, cover with water, and bring to a boil over high heat; boil for 3 minutes, then drain. Return nuts to pan and add milk, bay leaf, thyme, basil, and parsley. Heat to scalding; cover and set aside for 20 minutes.

Meanwhile, in a 3-quart pan, melt butter over medium heat. Add onion and celery and cook, stirring occasionally, until soft (about 10 minutes). Stir in flour and cook until bubbly. Gradually stir in stock; cook, stirring, until soup comes to a boil. Reduce heat and simmer gently, uncovered, for 10 minutes.

Remove bay leaf and add milk mixture to pan. Whirl stock mixture, a portion at a time, in a food processor or blender until smooth. Return to pan and heat until steaming; add sherry and season to taste with salt and pepper. Garnish individual servings with chives, if desired. Makes about 6 servings.

FRESH ASPARAGUS BISQUE

In spring, when asparagus is at its peak, take advantage of the bounty by serving this rich soup. It's a good starter for a dinner party—and equally appropriate for a family lunch.

    2 pounds asparagus
    2 tablespoons butter or margarine
    4 green onions (including tops), sliced
    1 small thin-skinned potato, peeled and
       diced
    6 cups Chicken Stock (page 5) or regular-
       strength canned chicken broth
    ½ teaspoon *each* salt, dill weed, and
       Worcestershire
    ⅛ teaspoon pepper
    2 egg yolks, beaten
    ½ cup whipping cream or half-and-half
       (light cream)
       Chopped chives or chopped parsley

Break off and discard white, fibrous ends of asparagus. Cut spears into 1-inch pieces; set aside.

In a 4 to 5-quart pan, melt butter over medium heat. Add onions and cook, stirring occasionally, until soft (about 3 minutes). Add potato, stock, salt, dill weed, Worcestershire, pepper, and asparagus. Reduce heat, cover, and simmer until vegetables are very tender (about 30 minutes).

Whirl vegetable mixture, a portion at a time, in a food processor or blender until smooth. Return to pan. Blend egg yolks and cream; stir into soup and heat, stirring, until steaming.

Garnish individual servings with chives. Makes about 6 servings.

CREAM OF ARTICHOKE SOUP

Fresh artichokes can be used to prepare many delightful dishes, from simple first courses to elegant entrées. Here they contribute to a creamy soup.

       Seasoned Artichokes (recipe follows)
    ¼ cup butter or margarine
    2 tablespoons chopped shallots
    1 teaspoon dry basil
    2 cups Chicken Stock (page 5) or regular-
       strength canned chicken broth
    ½ cup whipping cream
       Dry sherry

Prepare Seasoned Artichokes and let cool until easy to handle. Scrape and reserve pulp from leaves; discard leaves. Scoop out and discard fuzzy center from hearts and peel fibrous exterior of stems. Coarsely chop hearts and stems (you should have 3 cups).

In a 2 to 3-quart pan, melt butter over medium heat. Add shallots, basil, and artichoke pulp and hearts; stir until hot (about 3 minutes). Whirl artichoke mixture, a portion at a time, in a food processor or blender until smooth. Return to pan and add stock and cream; bring to a boil over medium-high heat, stirring constantly. Just before serving, add sherry to taste. Makes 4 servings.

Seasoned Artichokes. Immerse 4 large (about 5-inch diameter) **artichokes** in water; shake to dislodge foreign matter. Snap off small outer leaves. Cut off lower portion of stems, leaving about 1½ inches.

In a 6 to 8-quart pan, combine 4 quarts **water,** 2 tablespoons *each* **olive oil** and **white wine vinegar,** 1 **bay leaf,** 2 teaspoons **dry basil,** and ½ teaspoon **ground allspice.** Add artichokes. Cover and bring to a boil over high heat; reduce heat and simmer until bases of artichokes are tender when pierced (about 40 minutes). Lift out artichokes and drain well.

CHILLED AVOCADO SOUP

Quickly prepared, this cold soup relies on the natural sweetness and thick texture of ripe avocados; bacon and mild onion add crunch. The soup is best if allowed to chill for several hours before serving.

    2 large ripe avocados, pitted and peeled
    2 tablespoons lemon juice
    1 clove garlic
       About 5 cups Chicken Stock (page 5) or
       regular-strength canned chicken broth
    ½ pound bacon, crisply cooked, drained,
       and crumbled
    1 small red onion, finely chopped

Cut avocados into chunks and place in a food processor or blender along with lemon juice, garlic, and about 1 cup of the stock; whirl until smooth. Transfer avocado mixture to a bowl and blend in remaining stock (about 4 cups) until soup is desired consistency. Cover and refrigerate until well chilled.

Place bacon and onion in small serving bowls; pass at the table to sprinkle over individual servings. Makes about 6 servings.

Beet Borscht

Cold beet borscht is traditional in the cuisines of Russia and Poland. So appealing is its tangy sweet-and-sour flavor, however, that it has gained popularity worldwide.

        2 **pounds beets without tops**
           About 4 cups water
        1 **small onion, chopped**
        2 **eggs**
        2 **tablespoons sugar**
        3 **tablespoons lemon juice**
           Salt and pepper
           Lemon slices

Peel beets and coarsely shred in a food processor or through large holes of a grater (you should have about 5 cups). In a 4 to 5-quart pan, combine beets, 4 cups of the water, and onion. Bring to a boil over high heat; reduce heat, cover, and simmer until beets are tender to bite (about 15 minutes). Let cool. Add eggs, sugar, and lemon juice.

Whirl beet mixture, a portion at a time, in a food processor or blender until smooth. Season to taste with salt and pepper. Cover and refrigerate for at least 2 hours or up to 2 days.

Just before serving, stir borscht; if too thick to sip, add water to thin soup to desired consistency. Garnish individual servings with lemon slices. Makes about 6 servings.

Broccoli-Buttermilk Soup

Buttermilk lends a creamy texture and pleasant tartness—but few additional calories—to this soup.

           About 1 pound broccoli
        2 **cups Beef Stock (page 5) or regular-strength canned beef broth**
        1 **small onion, quartered**
        1 **bay leaf**
        1 **teaspoon dry basil**
        ½ **teaspoon sugar**
        1 **clove garlic**
       1¾ **cups buttermilk**
           Salt and pepper

Peel and slice broccoli stems; break tops into small flowerets. In a 3-quart pan, combine stems and flowerets, stock, onion, bay leaf, basil, sugar, and garlic. Bring to a boil over high heat; reduce heat, cover, and simmer until broccoli is tender (about 15 minutes). Discard bay leaf.

Whirl broccoli mixture, a portion at a time, in a food processor or blender until smooth. Return to pan and, with a wire whisk, beat in buttermilk; heat until steaming. Season to taste with salt and pepper. Makes 4 to 6 servings.

Curried Carrot Bisque

You can serve this well-seasoned carrot soup plain, or dress it up with a variety of condiments to make it festive enough for guests. The condiments also add interesting flavor accents and textural contrasts to the smooth purée.

        ¼ **cup butter or margarine**
        2 **cloves garlic, minced or pressed**
        2 **large onions, sliced**
        1 **teaspoon ground coriander**
        ¾ **teaspoon curry powder**
        ¼ **teaspoon ground ginger**
        ⅛ **teaspoon ground allspice**
        3 **tablespoons all-purpose flour**
        2 **cups water**
       1½ **pounds carrots, sliced**
        7 **chicken bouillon cubes**
        5 **cups milk**
           Salt
           Condiments (suggestions follow)

In a 5 to 6-quart pan, melt butter over medium heat. Add garlic, onions, coriander, curry powder, ginger, and allspice. Cook, stirring occasionally, until onions are very soft (about 15 minutes). Stir in flour until all vegetables are coated. Add water, carrots, and bouillon cubes. Bring to a boil over high heat; reduce heat, cover, and simmer until carrots are very tender (about 25 minutes).

Whirl carrot mixture, a portion at a time, in a food processor or blender until smooth (add enough of the milk for blender to run easily). Return to pan; add remaining milk and heat until steaming. Season to taste with salt.

If made ahead, reheat over medium-low heat, stirring occasionally; do not boil.

Place condiments of your choice in separate bowls; pass at the table to spoon over individual servings. Makes 8 to 10 servings.

Condiments. Choose from the following: **Roasted salted sunflower seeds,** chopped **hard-cooked eggs, plain yogurt,** and **fresh cilantro (coriander).**

ICED CARROT & ORANGE SOUP

Served ice-cold, this smooth golden blend of carrots and fresh orange juice will spark appetites before a summer barbecue. Offer the soup in chilled mugs to sip while the entrée is cooking over the coals.

        2 tablespoons butter or margarine
        1 pound carrots, thinly sliced
        1 large onion, sliced
        3 cups Chicken Stock (page 5) or regular-
          strength canned chicken broth
        1 teaspoon sugar
        ½ teaspoon dill weed
       1½ cups freshly squeezed orange juice
          Salt
          Grated orange peel (optional)

In a 3 to 4-quart pan, melt butter over medium heat. Add carrots and onion; cook, stirring occasionally, until onion is soft (about 10 minutes). Add stock, sugar, and dill weed. Bring to a boil over high heat; reduce heat, cover, and simmer until carrots are very tender (about 25 minutes).

Whirl carrot mixture, a portion at a time, in a food processor or blender until smooth. Stir in orange juice. Season to taste with salt. Cover and refrigerate for at least 4 hours or until next day. Stir well before serving.

Garnish individual servings with grated orange peel, if desired. Makes about 6 servings.

SMOOTH & CREAMY CARROT SOUP

Good carrot flavor, enhanced by the addition of cream, is the hallmark of this simple soup. The fancy carrot twist garnish adds an attractive touch; you can use it as a finishing accent on our other carrot soups, too.

        2 tablespoons butter or margarine
        1 large onion, finely chopped
        1 pound carrots, finely chopped
        2 tablespoons *each* tomato paste and
          long-grain white rice
        4 cups Chicken Stock (page 5) or regular-
          strength canned chicken broth
          Carrot Twists (directions follow) or
          parsley sprigs
        ½ cup whipping cream
          Salt and pepper

In a 3 to 4-quart pan, melt butter over medium heat. Add onion and cook, stirring occasionally, until soft (about 10 minutes). Add carrots, tomato paste, rice, and stock. Bring to a boil over high heat; reduce heat, cover, and simmer until carrots are very tender (about 25 minutes).

Meanwhile, prepare Carrot Twists; set aside for garnish.

Whirl carrot mixture, a portion at a time, in a food processor or blender until smooth. Return to pan; add cream and heat until steaming. Season to taste with salt and pepper.

Garnish individual servings with twists. Makes about 6 servings.

Carrot Twists. With a vegetable peeler, pare thin, 3-inch-long strips from a **carrot.** Cut a 1-inch length-wise slit in center of each strip, then soak in cold **salted water** for 10 minutes. Slip one end of strip through slit and pull back gently to form a twist.

CAULIFLOWER SOUP

Pictured on page 31

A golden swirl of melting butter and a light sprinkling of ground nutmeg crown this irresistible puréed vegetable soup.

        1 large head cauliflower (about 2 lbs.), green
          leaves removed
        3 cups Chicken Stock (page 5) or regular-
          strength canned chicken broth
        4 medium-size leeks (white parts only) or 1
          medium-size onion, chopped
        1 medium-size thin-skinned potato, peeled
          and diced
        2 chicken bouillon cubes
        ⅔ cup whipping cream
          Ground nutmeg
          Salt and white pepper
          Butter or margarine

Thinly slice cauliflower (you should have about 4 cups). In a 3-quart pan, combine stock, leeks, potato, bouillon cubes, and cauliflower. Bring to a boil over high heat; reduce heat, cover, and simmer until vegetables are soft (15 to 20 minutes).

Whirl cauliflower mixture, a portion at a time, in a food processor or blender until smooth. Return to pan. Add cream and ¼ teaspoon nutmeg. Season to taste with salt and white pepper, then heat until steaming.

Top individual servings with a small pat of butter, swirling lightly, and sprinkle with nutmeg. Makes about 6 servings.

CREAMED CELERY & GREEN ONION SOUP

Celery, a popular snack or appetizer when served raw, is also delicious when cooked with green onions and made into this creamy soup. A sprinkling of paprika adds color contrast.

1 bunch celery
2 bunches green onions (including tops)
1¼ cups water
¼ teaspoon thyme leaves
1 teaspoon salt
⅛ teaspoon pepper
2 tablespoons butter or margarine
2 tablespoons all-purpose flour
4 cups milk
Paprika

Rinse celery well; trim and set aside 5 stalks. Discard any bruised portions of remaining stalks; then dice (including leaves). Set 1 bunch of onions aside; dice remaining onions. Place diced onions and celery in a 3 to 4-quart pan; add water. Bring to a boil over high heat; reduce heat, cover, and simmer until vegetables are very soft (about 20 minutes).

Whirl celery mixture, a portion at a time, in a food processor or blender until smooth. Pour through a wire strainer and discard residue. Return to pan.

Dice reserved 5 stalks celery and cut reserved onions into ⅛ to ¼-inch slices. Add to celery mixture along with thyme, salt, and pepper and cook over medium heat just until tender.

In another 3 to 4-quart pan, melt butter over medium heat. Stir in flour and cook until bubbly (about 1 minute). Gradually stir in milk and cook, stirring, until thickened. Stir in celery mixture.

Sprinkle individual servings with paprika. Makes about 6 servings.

CHAYOTE SOUP

What looks like a wrinkled papaya, slices like a cucumber, tastes like summer squash when it's cooked, and is served as a vegetable? Answer: Chayote (pronounced chi-*yo*-dee). The fruit of a tropical vine originally from Latin America, chayote has a delicate flavor and firm, crisp flesh; its skin color ranges from light to dark green.

When you slice chayote for this soup, you can cut right through the soft, flat seed; it's edible and has a nutlike flavor.

1 tablespoon butter or margarine
1 small onion, chopped
4 cups Chicken Stock (page 5) or regular-strength canned chicken broth
1 large tomato, peeled, seeded, and chopped
¼ cup long-grain white rice
¾ teaspoon thyme leaves
½ teaspoon chili powder
¼ teaspoon liquid hot pepper seasoning
2 small chayotes (about 1 lb. *total*)
2 teaspoons all-purpose flour
¾ cup sour cream
Salt and pepper

In a 3 to 4-quart pan, melt butter over medium heat. Add onion and cook, stirring occasionally, until soft (about 10 minutes). Stir in stock, tomato, rice, thyme, chili powder, and hot pepper seasoning.

Scrub chayotes and cut into ½-inch cubes. Add to stock mixture. Bring to a boil over high heat; reduce heat, cover, and simmer until tender (20 to 25 minutes). Stir flour into sour cream; add to soup and heat, stirring, until steaming. Season to taste with salt and pepper. Makes 6 servings.

CURRIED CREAM OF CORN SOUP

Use fresh or frozen corn for this ultra-quick cream soup lightly seasoned with curry. Garnish each serving with parsley, croutons, or small pretzels.

2 tablespoons butter or margarine
4 cups corn, fresh or frozen and thawed
¼ medium-size onion, sliced
2 tablespoons all-purpose flour
¾ teaspoon curry powder
¼ teaspoon salt
Dash of pepper
2 cups Chicken Stock (page 5) or regular-strength canned chicken broth
2 cups milk

In a 3 to 4-quart pan, melt butter over medium heat. Add corn and onion and cook, stirring occasionally, until corn is tender (about 5 minutes). Stir in flour, curry powder, salt, and pepper; cook, stirring, for about 1 minute. Gradually stir in stock; cook, stirring, until bubbly and slightly thickened. Add milk.

Whirl corn mixture, a portion at a time, in a food processor or blender until smooth. Pour through a wire strainer; discard residue. Return to pan; heat until steaming. Makes 4 or 5 servings.

18

S parkling cubes of consommé make a refreshing first course, especially when crowned with avocado and sour cream for Avocado Madrilène (page 11). Homemade Cheese Twists (page 58) are a tasty accompaniment.

SWEET & SOUR CRANBERRY SOUP

Similar in flavor and color to beet borscht (page 15), this tangy soup features cranberries and red cabbage in place of beets.

> 1 package (12 oz.) cranberries (about 2 cups)
> 7 cups water
> 1 small onion, chopped
> 1 large carrot, thinly sliced
> 5 beef bouillon cubes
> ⅓ to ½ cup firmly packed brown sugar
> 3 cups thinly shredded red cabbage
> Salt and pepper

In a 4-quart pan, combine cranberries with 1 cup of the water; cover and cook over medium-high heat until cranberries pop and start to fall apart. Mash with a potato masher or large spoon.

Add onion, carrot, bouillon cubes, remaining 6 cups water, and ⅓ cup of the sugar to cranberries. Bring to a boil over high heat; reduce heat to medium, cover, and cook for 20 minutes. Stir in cabbage and cook until tender (about 15 more minutes). If a sweeter flavor is desired, add more sugar; season to taste with salt and pepper. Makes about 6 servings.

CREAMY CROOKNECK SQUASH SOUP

Fresh summer squash and chives are quickly combined to make a chilled soup that's creamy but low in calories. Dieters will appreciate it, as will gardeners with burgeoning squash patches.

> 2 tablespoons butter or margarine
> 1 small onion, chopped
> 1 clove garlic, minced or pressed
> 4 cups thinly sliced crookneck squash
> 3 cups Chicken Stock (page 5) or regular-strength canned chicken broth
> 2 tablespoons finely minced fresh or freeze-dried chives
> ¼ teaspoon white pepper
> ¼ to ½ cup milk
> Salt
> Roasted sunflower seeds

In a 3 to 4-quart pan, melt butter over medium heat. Add onion and garlic and cook, stirring occasionally, until onion is soft (about 10 minutes). Add squash and stock. Bring to a boil over high heat; reduce heat, cover, and simmer just until squash is tender (about 5 minutes).

Whirl squash mixture, a portion at a time, in a food processor or blender until smooth. Stir in chives, pepper, and enough milk to achieve desired consistency. Season to taste with salt. Cover and refrigerate until well chilled. Serve cold; sprinkle sunflower seeds over individual servings. Makes about 6 servings.

DILLED CUCUMBER SOUP

This creamy cucumber soup is quick to prepare and can be served hot or cold, making it appropriate for a variety of occasions. It's seasoned with dill, which enhances the cucumber's fresh flavor.

> 2 large cucumbers (about 1 lb. *total*)
> 2 tablespoons butter or margarine
> ⅓ cup *each* finely chopped onion and green bell pepper
> ¼ cup all-purpose flour
> 2 cups Beef Stock (page 5) or regular-strength canned beef broth
> 2 cups milk
> 2 tablespoons minced fresh dill or 2 teaspoons dill weed
> 1 tablespoon Worcestershire
> ½ teaspoon *each* salt and ground nutmeg
> ¼ teaspoon pepper
> 2 tablespoons chopped parsley
> ⅓ cup thinly sliced green onions (including tops)

Peel cucumbers and cut into quarters lengthwise. With a small spoon, scoop out any large seeds; then cut crosswise into ⅛-inch-thick slices. Set aside.

In a 3-quart pan, melt butter over medium heat. Add chopped onion and bell pepper and cook, stirring occasionally, until onion is soft (about 10 minutes). Add flour and cook, stirring, until bubbly. Remove from heat and gradually stir in stock.

Return to heat and cook, stirring, until stock mixture comes to a boil. Add cucumber slices, milk, dill, Worcestershire, salt, nutmeg, and pepper. Continue cooking until cucumber mixture simmers, then cover and simmer, stirring occasionally, until cucumbers are tender but still slightly crisp (about 10 minutes). Stir in parsley. Serve warm. Or let cool; cover, refrigerate until well chilled, and serve cold.

Garnish individual servings with green onion slices. Makes about 6 servings.

ROASTED EGGPLANT SOUP

Very low in calories but high in fresh vegetable flavor, this eggplant soup is crowned with thin slivers of sweet red bell pepper. Busy cooks will appreciate its simple preparation.

    1 large eggplant (about 1½ lbs.), pierced in
      several places with a fork
    1 small onion
    3 cups Chicken Stock (page 5) or regular-
      strength canned chicken broth
    2 tablespoons lemon juice
      Salt and pepper
    8 or 12 thin red bell pepper slices
      Finely chopped parsley

Place eggplant and unpeeled onion in an 8 or 9-inch baking pan. Bake in a 400° oven until vegetables are very soft when squeezed (about 1¼ hours). Let cool, then peel.

Whirl vegetables, a portion at a time, in a food processor or blender until smooth. Transfer vegetable mixture to a 2 to 3-quart pan and blend in stock. Bring to a boil over high heat; add lemon juice and season to taste with salt and pepper.

Garnish individual servings with bell pepper slices and parsley. Makes 4 servings.

CREAM OF GARLIC SOUP

Rich and creamy soup flavored with just enough garlic to delight the palate—but not enough to overwhelm—is an unusual way to start a meal. Try it for company; you'll find that even those who think they don't like garlic will ask for a second helping. The soup goes together quickly but should be served immediately, so plan the rest of your menu accordingly.

    3 tablespoons butter or margarine
    2 teaspoons minced or pressed garlic (about
      4 large cloves)
    3 tablespoons all-purpose flour
    2 cans (10¾ oz. *each*) condensed chicken
      broth
    2 cups half-and-half (light cream)
      Dash of paprika
      Salt
    1 egg yolk
      Chopped parsley

In a 2 to 3-quart pan, melt butter over medium heat. Add garlic and cook, stirring, until soft but not browned (about 2 minutes). Stir in flour and cook until bubbly (about 1 minute). Gradually stir in broth and bring to a boil, stirring often.

Stir in half-and-half and paprika; season to taste with salt. Heat until steaming (do not boil). In a small bowl, beat egg yolk lightly; stir a small amount of the hot soup into egg yolk. Return egg yolk mixture to pan, stirring constantly.

Immediately ladle soup into individual bowls; garnish each with parsley. Makes about 4 servings.

CREAM OF LETTUCE SOUP

Lettuce has culinary potential that extends beyond the salad bowl, as this simple and unusual soup demonstrates.

    4 cups Chicken Stock (page 5) or regular-
      strength canned chicken broth
    4 cups firmly packed chopped butter lettuce
      or green leaf lettuce
    ¼ cup butter or margarine
    1 cup half-and-half (light cream)
      Salt and white pepper
      Chopped parsley
      Lemon wedges

Pour stock into a 2½ or 3-quart pan; bring to a boil over high heat. Stir in lettuce; reduce heat, cover, and simmer until lettuce is completely limp (8 to 10 minutes).

Whirl lettuce mixture, a portion at a time, with butter in a food processor or blender until smooth. Return to pan, stir in half-and-half, and heat, stirring constantly, until steaming. Season to taste with salt and pepper.

Garnish with parsley; pass lemon wedges at the table to squeeze into individual servings. Makes about 6 servings.

MINTED GREEN PEA BISQUE

A hint of mint accents the garden fresh flavor of this cold green pea soup. Served in attractive mugs, it makes an ideal first course for guests to sip at a summer party. Let the soup chill for at least 6 hours, or make it a day or two ahead, so the flavors have time

SEASONED CROUTONS

Garnishing possibilities for a bowl of soup are many and varied—a dollop of sour cream, a sprinkling of minced chives, a pat of butter, a sprig of mint—and all have their charm. But few garnishes are more appealing than a handful of crisp, buttery homemade croutons. They're easy to make from leftover French bread, and with the following recipe you can choose from among three flavor variations: herb and cheese, herb and onion, and garlic.

About ⅓ of a 1-pound loaf
day-old French bread
¼ cup butter or margarine
Italian Herb & Cheese,
Herb & Onion, or Garlic
Seasoning Mix (recipes
follow)

Cut bread into ½-inch cubes (you should have 2 cups *total*). Evenly spread on a rimmed baking sheet. Bake in a 300° oven for 10 minutes. Remove from oven and set aside; reduce oven temperature to 275°.

In a wide frying pan, melt butter over medium heat. Stir in seasoning mix of your choice. Add bread cubes and toss to coat evenly. Spread bread cubes out on baking sheet and bake until crisp and lightly browned (about 30 minutes). Let cool completely; store in a covered jar. Makes 2 cups.

Italian Herb & Cheese Seasoning Mix. Stir into melted butter ½ teaspoon **Worcestershire;** add 1 teaspoon **Italian herb seasoning** or ¼ teaspoon *each* dry basil and oregano, thyme, and marjoram leaves. Remove from heat and stir in 1 tablespoon grated **Parmesan cheese.**

Herb & Onion Seasoning Mix. Stir into melted butter 1 teaspoon **onion powder** and ½ teaspoon *each* **dry basil, dry chervil,** and **oregano leaves.** Remove from heat.

Garlic Seasoning Mix. Stir into melted butter 1 large clove **garlic,** minced or pressed, and 1 teaspoon **parsley flakes.** Remove from heat.

to blend and mellow. Meanwhile, you can chill the mugs, too.

1 tablespoon finely chopped onion
¼ cup shredded carrot
1 package (10 oz.) frozen peas
1 fresh mint sprig (about 3 inches long), crushed
1 teaspoon sugar
Dash of ground nutmeg
2 cups Chicken Stock (page 5) or regular-strength canned chicken broth
1 cup milk or half-and-half (light cream)
Salt and pepper
Chopped fresh mint (optional)

In a 2 to 3-quart pan, combine onion, carrot, peas, mint sprig, sugar, nutmeg, and stock. Bring to a boil over high heat; reduce heat, cover, and simmer until vegetables are very tender to bite (about 25 minutes).

Whirl pea mixture, a portion at a time, in a food processor or blender until smooth. Return to pan, stir in milk, and season to taste with salt and pepper.

Cover and refrigerate soup for at least 6 hours or until next day.

Just before serving, stir soup well, then pour into small chilled mugs. Garnish individual servings with chopped mint, if desired. Makes 4 servings.

LEEK BISQUE

One of the most elegant members of the onion family is the leek. When it's made into a soup or served as a vegetable, its delicate onion flavor adds interest to any meal.

- 5 large leeks (about 2 lbs. *total*)
- ¼ cup butter or margarine
- 2 medium-size carrots, thinly sliced
- 2 cloves garlic, minced or pressed
- ¾ cup chopped parsley
- 2 teaspoons *each* grated lemon peel and marjoram leaves
- ⅛ teaspoon white pepper
- 7 chicken bouillon cubes
- ½ cup water
- ¼ cup all-purpose flour
- 8 cups milk
- Condiments (optional; suggestions follow)

Trim and discard ends and tops of leeks, leaving about 3 inches of green leaves. Discard tough outer leaves. Split leeks in half lengthwise; rinse well, then thinly slice.

In a 5 to 6-quart pan, melt butter over medium heat. Add leeks, carrots, garlic, parsley, lemon peel, marjoram, pepper, bouillon cubes, and water. Bring to a boil over high heat; reduce heat, cover, and simmer, stirring occasionally, until vegetables are very tender (about 10 minutes). Stir in flour.

Whirl leek mixture, a portion at a time, in a food processor or blender until smooth (add enough of the milk for blender to run easily). Return to pan; add remaining milk and heat, stirring often, until steaming.

If desired, serve with condiments of your choice to sprinkle over individual servings. Makes 8 to 10 servings.

Condiments. Choose from the following: Toasted **sliced almonds,** crumbled crisply cooked **bacon, croutons** (homemade, page 21, or purchased), and thinly sliced raw **leek stems.**

KOHLRABI BISQUE

Add a fresh touch to your menus by making soup out of unusual vegetables. This smooth, pale green bisque is prepared with kohlrabi, which gives the soup a flavor somewhere in between broccoli and turnips. (If you prefer, you can use broccoli in place of the kohlrabi.)

- About 2¼ pounds kohlrabi or broccoli
- 3 tablespoons butter or margarine
- 1 large onion, finely chopped
- 1 clove garlic, minced or pressed
- 2 tablespoons all-purpose flour
- 6 cups Chicken Stock (page 5) or regular-strength canned chicken broth
- 1 teaspoon marjoram leaves
- ¼ teaspoon white pepper
- ½ cup finely chopped parsley
- Salt

Discard kohlrabi leaves and stems. Peel bulbs to remove tough outer skin. (For broccoli, cut flowerets off stalks; trim and discard stalk ends, then peel stalks.) Cut vegetable into ½-inch cubes.

In a 5 to 6-quart pan, melt butter over medium heat. Add onion and garlic and cook, stirring occasionally, until onion is soft (about 10 minutes). Add flour and cook, stirring, until bubbly. Blend in 3 cups of the stock, marjoram, and pepper. Bring to a boil. Add vegetable cubes; reduce heat, cover, and simmer until tender when pierced (25 to 35 minutes for kohlrabi, 10 to 15 minutes for broccoli).

Add chopped parsley and remaining 3 cups stock. Whirl vegetable mixture, a portion at a time, in a food processor or blender until smooth. If desired, pour through a wire strainer and discard residue. Return to pan; heat until steaming. Season to taste with salt. Makes 8 to 10 servings.

MUSHROOM VELVET SOUP

The nutty flavor of sautéed mushrooms marries well with tangy sour cream in this puréed soup.

- ¼ cup butter or margarine
- ½ pound mushrooms, sliced
- ½ cup finely chopped parsley
- 1 medium-size onion, chopped
- 1 tablespoon all-purpose flour
- 2 cups Beef Stock (page 5) or regular-strength canned beef broth
- 1 cup sour cream

In a 2½ or 3-quart pan, melt butter over medium heat. Add mushrooms, parsley, and onion and cook, stirring occasionally, until all liquid has evaporated (about 5 minutes). Stir in flour and cook for about 1 minute; gradually blend in stock and bring to a boil, stirring. Whirl mushroom mixture and sour cream, a portion at a time, in a food processor or blender until smooth. Return to pan; heat until steaming. Makes 4 servings.

For an elegant company dinner, dress up each serving of Add-on Vichyssoise (page 29) with caviar. On less formal occasions, slivered ham and ground nutmeg step in as flavorful substitutes.

MUSHROOM SOUP PAPRIKA

Paprika adds warm color and flavor to this mellow mushroom soup brimming with thin mushroom slices; a final swirl of egg yolk and sour cream lends a silken touch.

> 1 tablespoon butter or margarine
> ½ pound mushrooms, thinly sliced
> 1 teaspoon paprika
> 1 tablespoon all-purpose flour
> 2 tablespoons finely chopped parsley
> 4 cups Beef Stock (page 5) or regular-strength canned beef broth
> 1 egg yolk
> 1 cup sour cream

In a 2 to 3-quart pan, melt butter over medium heat. Add mushrooms and paprika and cook, stirring occasionally, until mushrooms are soft and all liquid has evaporated (about 5 minutes). Stir in flour and cook, stirring, for about 1 minute; then add parsley. Gradually stir in stock. Bring to a boil over high heat; reduce heat, cover, and simmer for 30 minutes.

In a soup tureen, beat together egg yolk and sour cream. Gradually stir in hot soup. Makes about 6 servings.

DRIED MUSHROOM SOUP

European mushrooms—porcini, chanterelles, and others—are increasingly popular in today's kitchens. For this creamy soup, you can use them in their dried form. Look for dried mushrooms in a delicatessen or gourmet shop.

> 4 packages (about ⁷⁄₁₆ oz. *each*) dried European mushrooms
> 2 cups hot water
> 3 tablespoons butter or margarine
> 1 large onion, finely chopped
> 3 tablespoons all-purpose flour
> 1 cup half-and-half (light cream)
> ⅛ teaspoon pepper
> About 2 cups milk
> Salt

Soak mushrooms (you should have about 1½ cups) in hot water until pliable (about 30 minutes). Lift out mushrooms with a slotted spoon and pour soaking liquid (except for residue at bottom) into a small pan. Add mushrooms (snip off any tough stems and chop any large pieces). Bring to a boil over high heat; reduce heat, cover, and simmer until tender when pierced (about 20 minutes).

Meanwhile, in a 3-quart pan, melt butter over medium heat. Add onion and cook, stirring occasionally, until very soft (about 15 minutes). Add flour and cook, stirring, until just slightly browned. Gradually stir in half-and-half and cook, stirring, until onion mixture is bubbly and thickened.

Stir in mushroom mixture, then add pepper and 2 cups of the milk. Season to taste with salt; heat until steaming. If desired, add more milk to thin to desired consistency. Serve immediately. Makes about 6 servings.

CREAM OF PARSNIP SOUP

There's nothing like hot soup to chase away the winter chills, and winter vegetables such as parsnips make delightful soups. This one is smooth and well seasoned, and topped with crisp, buttery croutons.

> 2 cups Herb & Onion Seasoned Croutons (page 21) *or* ¼ cup butter or margarine plus 2 cups purchased herb-seasoned croutons
> 2 pounds parsnips
> 1 large onion, chopped
> 3½ cups Chicken Stock (page 5) or regular-strength canned chicken broth
> 2¼ teaspoons dry basil
> 2½ cups milk
> 2 tablespoons chopped parsley
> Salt, pepper, and garlic salt

Prepare Herb & Onion Seasoned Croutons. (Or melt butter in a small frying pan over medium heat; add purchased croutons and cook, stirring often, until lightly toasted.) Set aside.

Peel parsnips and thinly slice; place in a 3 to 4-quart pan along with onion, stock, and basil. Bring to a boil over high heat; reduce heat, cover, and simmer until parsnips mash easily (about 15 minutes).

Whirl vegetable mixture, a portion at a time, in a food processor or blender until smooth. Return to pan, add milk and parsley, and heat until steaming, stirring occasionally. Season to taste with salt, pepper, and garlic salt.

Evenly top individual servings with croutons. Makes 6 to 8 servings.

PARSNIP & CARROT SOUP

White wine, shallots, and cream flavor the broth for this soup; they make an elegant foil for the earthy sweetness of parsnips and carrots.

- 6 tablespoons butter or margarine
- 2 tablespoons finely chopped shallots or green onion (including top)
- 3 medium-size carrots, cut into chunks
- 2 medium-size parsnips (about ¾ lb. *total*), peeled and cut into chunks
- 3 cups Chicken Stock (page 5) or regular-strength canned chicken broth
- ½ cup dry white wine
- ½ cup half-and-half (light cream)
  Chopped chives
  Ground cinnamon

In a 3 to 4-quart pan, melt 2 tablespoons of the butter over medium-high heat. Add shallots and cook, stirring, until shallots begin to look translucent (about 3 minutes). Add carrots, parsnips, and stock. Bring to a boil over high heat; reduce heat, cover, and simmer until vegetables mash easily (about 15 minutes).

Whirl parsnip mixture, a portion at a time, in a food processor or blender until smooth. Return to pan, stir in wine and half-and-half, and heat until steaming.

Dot individual servings with remaining 4 tablespoons butter, then sprinkle with chives and dust with cinnamon. Makes 4 to 6 servings.

SNOW PEA SOUP

Quick to make, this light, smooth, emerald-tinted soup uses Chinese pea pods, showcasing their delicate flavor in a broth base. First you sauté the peas briefly to bring out their sweetness and help stabilize their color; after the peas simmer in broth, you purée the soup and strain it to remove any fibers.

- ¼ cup butter or margarine
- 1 cup chopped green onions (including tops)
- 1½ pounds Chinese pea pods (also called snow or sugar peas) or sugar snap peas, ends and strings removed
- 4 cups Chicken Stock (page 5) or regular-strength canned chicken broth
- 1 cup whipping cream or plain yogurt
  Plain yogurt or sour cream

In a 5 to 6-quart pan, melt butter over medium-high heat; add onions and pea pods and cook, stirring constantly, until pea pods turn a brighter green (3 to 5 minutes). Lift out 12 to 18 pea pods and set aside. Add stock and bring to a boil over high heat; reduce heat and simmer, uncovered, until pea pods are very tender to bite (about 20 minutes).

Whirl pea pod mixture, a portion at a time, in a food processor or blender until smooth; then, with back of a spoon, firmly rub through a wire strainer and discard residue. Return to pan; stir in cream and heat, stirring, until steaming.

Garnish individual servings with reserved pea pods and a spoonful of yogurt. Makes 4 to 6 servings.

CREAM OF SORREL SOUP

Scarcely known in this country, sorrel is a staple in French cooking (the French word for sorrel is *oseille*) and in eastern European and Jewish cuisines (where it's known as *schav*). Tasting like a sharp, sprightly spinach, sorrel is available in some markets and is cultivated by many home gardeners. It can be eaten raw or cooked; those who enjoy its tangy flavor will want to try it in this soup.

Before using sorrel, clean it well. Tear off and discard any tough stems and center ribs; rinse the leaves and pat them dry.

- 3 tablespoons butter or margarine
- 1 medium-size onion, chopped
- 1 medium-size potato, peeled and diced
- 3½ cups Chicken Stock (page 5) or regular-strength canned chicken broth
- 4 cups finely shredded sorrel
- ⅓ cup whipping cream
  Salt and pepper
  Ground nutmeg or sour cream

In a 4-quart pan, melt butter over medium heat. Add onion and cook, stirring occasionally, until soft (about 10 minutes). Stir in potato and stock. Bring to a boil over high heat; reduce heat, cover, and simmer until potato mashes easily (about 20 minutes). Stir in sorrel and cook for 3 minutes.

Whirl sorrel mixture, a portion at a time, in a food processor or blender until smooth. Return to pan, stir in cream, and season to taste with salt and pepper. Heat until steaming.

Serve warm, dusting individual servings with ground nutmeg. Or let cool; cover, refrigerate until well chilled, and serve cold with a dollop of sour cream. Makes 4 to 6 servings.

Ladled from a pumpkin shell and sprinkled with freshly grated nutmeg, Autumn Squash Soup (facing page) makes a warming walk-around first course for guests to sip at a football buffet, Halloween party, or other seasonal gathering.

• AUTUMN SQUASH SOUP •

Pictured on facing page

Hard-shelled winter squash such as pumpkins make delicious, nutty-tasting soups for cool-weather enjoyment. For this one, you can use a hollowed-out pumpkin shell as a festive serving container; make the soup itself from pumpkin or another winter squash of your choice.

    ¼ cup salad oil
    4 medium-size onions, chopped
    2 teaspoons thyme leaves
       About ½ teaspoon ground nutmeg
    1 pound rutabagas, peeled and diced
    2 pounds thin-skinned potatoes, peeled and cubed
       About 8 pounds squash (banana, butternut, Hubbard, pumpkin, or acorn), peeled and cubed (16 cups)
   14 cups Chicken Stock (page 5) or regular-strength canned chicken broth
    1 large pumpkin shell (about 6-qt. capacity), top cut off and inside scraped clean (optional)
       Boiling water (optional)

In an 8 to 10-quart pan, combine oil, onions, thyme, and ½ teaspoon of the nutmeg; cook over medium-high heat, stirring often, until onions are soft (about 5 minutes).

Add rutabagas, potatoes, and squash; cook over medium heat, stirring occasionally, until vegetables begin to soften (about 30 minutes). Pour in stock and bring to a boil over high heat. Reduce heat, cover, and simmer until squash mashes easily (about 1½ hours).

Meanwhile, heat pumpkin shell, if desired, by filling it with boiling water; let stand until shell feels warm (about 20 minutes). Drain water.

While shell is heating, whirl squash mixture, a portion at a time, in a food processor or blender until smooth. Return to pan and bring to a boil over medium-high heat, stirring often.

Pour soup into shell, if used. Serve in cups or mugs, and sprinkle individual servings with nutmeg. Makes 12 to 16 servings.

• HOT SENEGALESE SOUP •

Chicken broth, curried vegetables, and cream are the basis of Senegalese soup, which is usually served chilled. This hot version also contains applesauce and is further distinguished by a coriander-cream topping.

    3 tablespoons butter or margarine
    ½ cup finely chopped celery
    ¼ cup finely chopped onion
    ½ teaspoon curry powder
    2 tablespoons all-purpose flour
    ¾ cup unsweetened applesauce
    2 cups Chicken Stock (page 5) or regular-strength canned chicken broth
    2 cups half-and-half (light cream)
       Salt
    ¾ cup whipping cream
    ¼ teaspoon ground coriander

In a 2 to 3-quart pan, melt butter over medium heat. Add celery and onion and cook, stirring occasionally, until very soft (8 to 10 minutes). Blend in curry powder and flour; cook for 1 to 2 minutes. Gradually stir in applesauce, stock, and half-and-half. Heat until steaming. Season to taste with salt and pour into individual ovenproof bowls.

In a small bowl, softly whip cream; stir in coriander. Spoon evenly over soup. Broil about 6 inches below heat until cream is golden (1 to 2 minutes). Serve immediately. Makes 4 or 5 servings.

• TOMATO SOUP •

Pictured on page 31

A trio of toppings—Swiss cheese, sour cream, and croutons—embellishes this colorful tomato soup.

    1 cup Herb & Onion Seasoned Croutons (page 21)
    3 tablespoons butter or margarine, melted
    1 medium-size onion, cut into chunks
    1 can (6 oz.) tomato paste
    4 cups Chicken Stock (page 5) or regular-strength canned chicken broth
    1 large tomato, finely chopped (reserve juice)
       Salt
    1 cup (4 oz.) shredded Swiss cheese
    1 cup sour cream

Prepare Herb & Onion Seasoned Croutons and set aside.

Whirl butter, onion, and tomato paste in a food processor or blender until smooth. Pour into a 3 to 4-quart pan and bring to a vigorous boil over high heat, stirring constantly. Add stock and tomato, including juice. Heat until steaming. Season to taste with salt.

Place Swiss cheese, sour cream, and croutons in separate bowls; pass at the table to spoon over individual servings. Makes 4 servings.

FRESH TOMATO SOUP WITH BASIL

Nothing accents the sweet ripeness of tomato better than the pungent flavor of fresh basil. While both are in season, you might serve this soup, a smooth blend of tomatoes with other fresh vegetables.

        3   tablespoons butter or margarine
        1   large onion, sliced
        1   medium-size carrot, shredded
        4   large ripe tomatoes, peeled, seeded, and coarsely chopped (about 4 cups)
        ½   cup packed fresh basil leaves
        1   teaspoon salt
        ¾   teaspoon sugar
        ⅛   teaspoon white pepper
        2   cups Chicken Stock (page 5) or regular-strength chicken broth
        1   tablespoon tiny soup pasta (pastina)

In a 3-quart pan, melt butter over medium heat. Add onion and carrot and cook, stirring occasionally, until onion is soft (about 10 minutes). Stir in tomatoes, basil, salt, sugar, and pepper. Increase heat to medium-high and bring to a boil, stirring constantly; reduce heat, cover, and simmer for 10 minutes. Whirl tomato mixture, a portion at a time, in a food processor or blender until smooth; set aside.

Pour stock into pan and bring to a boil over high heat. Add soup pasta, reduce heat to medium, and cook until tender (about 7 minutes). Stir in tomato mixture and heat until steaming. Makes 4 servings.

• FREEZER TOMATO SOUP •

If you grow your own tomatoes, they may ripen faster than you can keep up with them. One good way to preserve the surplus so you can enjoy the flavor of vine-ripened tomatoes later is to make soup, then store it in the freezer.

This recipe makes a smooth, thick purée that, after thawing, is ready to heat and eat; for variety, you can blend the tomato base with milk or cream.

    7 to 8   pounds fully ripe tomatoes (16 to 18 large)
        3   large onions, finely chopped
        ¼   cup each sugar and chopped parsley
        6   tablespoons each cornstarch and water
            Salt and pepper
            Dash of ground cloves (optional)
            Butter or sour cream

Core tomatoes, then chop enough to make 12 cups. In a 6 to 8-quart pan, combine tomatoes, onions, sugar, and parsley. Cook over medium heat, stirring often, until tomatoes make juice and mixture comes to a boil. Reduce heat to medium-low, cover, and cook for 45 minutes, stirring occasionally.

Stir together cornstarch and water; add to tomato mixture and cook, stirring, until mixture boils and thickens. Remove from heat and press mixture, a portion at a time, through a wire strainer; discard seeds and pulp. Let cool, then pour into freezer containers, leaving about an inch for expansion at top. Cover and freeze for up to 6 months.

To serve, thaw soup, pour into a pan over medium heat, and heat, stirring, until steaming. Season to taste with salt, pepper, and, if desired, cloves. Top individual servings with a small pat of butter. Makes about 12 servings.

CREAM OF TOMATO SOUP

To each pint of thawed **Freezer Tomato Soup,** add 1 cup **milk** or half-and-half (light cream) and ½ teaspoon **dry basil.** Heat and serve as directed above.

CHILLED VEGETABLE BISQUE

Carrots, leeks, potatoes, and watercress all contribute to the fresh vegetable flavor of this cold soup.

      1½   cups diced carrots
        2   cups each thinly sliced leeks and peeled, diced thin-skinned potatoes
      3½   cups Chicken Stock (page 5) or regular-strength canned chicken broth
        1   cup loosely packed chopped watercress
    ½ to ¾   cup milk
            Salt, pepper, and ground nutmeg
            Thinly sliced green onion (including top)
            Crumbled crisply cooked bacon

In a 3-quart pan, combine carrots, leeks, potatoes, and 2 cups of the stock. Bring to a boil over high heat; reduce heat, cover, and simmer until vegetables are tender (about 15 minutes). Add watercress and cook for 2 minutes; stir in remaining 1½ cups stock.

Whirl carrot mixture, a portion at a time, in a food processor or blender until smooth. Stir in enough milk to thin to desired consistency; season to taste with salt, pepper, and nutmeg. Cover and refrigerate until well chilled. Garnish with onion and bacon. Makes 6 to 8 servings.

CREAMY VEGETABLE SOUP

Diced apple and sliced banana add fruity overtones to this vegetable soup, lightly seasoned with curry. For fewer calories, substitute 1 cup of plain yogurt plus 1 teaspoon of sugar for the sour cream.

> 2 tablespoons butter or margarine
> 1 medium-size onion, chopped
> 1 teaspoon curry powder
> 6 cups Chicken Stock (page 5) or regular-strength canned chicken broth
> 1 medium-size thin-skinned potato, peeled and diced (about 1½ cups)
> 2 cups sliced celery
> 1 tart apple, peeled and diced
> ½ medium-size banana, peeled and sliced
> 1 cup sour cream
> Minced chives or sliced green onion tops

In a 5 to 6-quart pan, melt butter over medium heat. Add onion and cook, stirring occasionally, until very soft (about 15 minutes). Stir in curry powder and cook for 1 minute. Add stock, potato, celery, apple, and banana. Bring to a boil over high heat; reduce heat, cover, and simmer until vegetables are very soft (about 30 minutes). Remove from heat and stir in sour cream.

Whirl soup, a portion at a time, in a food processor or blender until smooth. Return to pan and heat until steaming. Serve hot. Or let cool; cover, refrigerate until well chilled, and serve cold. Garnish individual servings with chives. Makes about 10 servings.

VEGETABLE SOUP

Pictured on page 31

Winter vegetables abound in this thick and savory soup. Potato, turnip, onion, leek, and carrot all help thicken the purée.

> 2 tablespoons butter or margarine
> 1 large onion, chopped
> 1 large leek (white part only), sliced
> About 6 cups Chicken Stock (page 5) or regular-strength canned chicken broth
> 1 *each* medium-size thin-skinned potato and turnip, peeled and diced
> 8 medium-size carrots, thinly sliced
> ¼ teaspoon thyme leaves
> Salt
> Whipped cream or sour cream (optional)

In a 3-quart pan, melt butter over medium heat. Add onion and leek; cook, stirring occasionally, until soft (about 10 minutes). Add 6 cups of the stock, potato, turnip, carrots, and thyme. Bring to a boil over high heat; reduce heat, cover, and simmer until vegetables are very soft (about 20 minutes).

Whirl carrot mixture, a portion at a time, in a food processor or blender until smooth. Return to pan, season to taste with salt, and thin with additional stock, if desired. Heat until steaming. Serve hot. Or let cool; cover, refrigerate until well chilled, and serve cold. Garnish individual servings with whipped cream, if desired. Makes 6 to 8 servings.

ADD-ON VICHYSSOISE

Pictured on page 23

The cold potato and leek soup called vichyssoise has long been a favorite of discriminating diners. Here's a fresh version that you top with slivered ham and nutmeg for everyday meals, with caviar for special occasions.

> 5 medium-size leeks
> ½ cup (¼ lb.) butter or margarine
> 1 medium-size onion, coarsely chopped
> 4 medium-size thin-skinned potatoes, peeled and cut into chunks
> 5½ cups Beef Stock (page 5) or regular-strength canned beef broth
> 1 cucumber, peeled, seeded, and cut into chunks
> 1 cup *each* plain yogurt and sour cream
> 36 to 40 whole chives
> 1 pound boiled ham, slivered (optional)
> Ground nutmeg (optional)
> Red or black caviar (optional)

Trim and discard ends and tops of leeks, leaving about 3 inches of green leaves. Discard tough outer leaves. Split leeks in half lengthwise; rinse well, then coarsely chop.

In a 5 to 6-quart pan, melt butter over medium heat. Add leeks and onion and cook, stirring often, until leeks are very soft and slightly tinged with brown (about 30 minutes). Add potatoes, stock, and cucumber. Bring to a boil over high heat; reduce heat, cover, and simmer until potatoes mash easily (about 25 minutes). Let cool to lukewarm.

Whirl leek mixture, yogurt, and sour cream, a portion at a time, in a blender until smooth. Cover and refrigerate until well chilled. Garnish individual servings with chives and, if desired, either with ham and nutmeg or with caviar. Makes 8 to 10 servings.

• WATERCRESS SOUP •

Pictured on facing page

This soup owes its brilliant green color to one extra step in its preparation: blanching and chilling the vegetable before adding it to the soup. This prevents any dulling of the color by heat.

    5   cups Chicken Stock (page 5) or regular-
        strength canned chicken broth
    1   medium-size thin-skinned potato, peeled
        and coarsely chopped
    2   medium-size onions, coarsely chopped
    1   cup firmly packed watercress sprigs
        Boiling water
        Ice water
        Salt and white pepper
    2   to 4 tablespoons whipping cream
        Watercress sprigs

In a 3-quart pan, bring stock to a boil over high heat. Add potato and onions; reduce heat, cover, and simmer until potato is very soft when pierced (about 20 minutes).

Immerse the 1 cup watercress in boiling water, drain at once, and immerse in ice water just long enough to chill; drain again.

Whirl onion mixture and watercress, a portion at a time, in a food processor or blender until smooth. Return to pan and heat until steaming. Season to taste with salt and pepper, and stir in cream.

Garnish individual servings with watercress sprigs. Makes about 6 servings.

• CHILLED ZUCCHINI BISQUE •

While the chef is busy at the barbecue, treat your guests to cold mugs of soup made from zucchini. Enriched with cream, the soup is subtly seasoned with nutmeg to enhance the flavor of the vegetable; if you desire a garnish, you can add an additional sprinkling of nutmeg on top.

    ¼   cup butter or margarine
    1   medium-size onion, chopped
    5   medium-size zucchini (about 1¼ lbs.
        total), thinly sliced
    3½ cups Chicken Stock (page 5) or regular-
        strength canned chicken broth
    ½   cup half-and-half (light cream)
    ⅛   teaspoon *each* salt and pepper
        About ¼ teaspoon ground nutmeg

In a 3 to 4-quart pan, melt butter over medium heat. Add onion and zucchini and cook, stirring occasionally, until soft (about 10 minutes). Add stock and bring to a boil over high heat; reduce heat, cover, and simmer until vegetables are tender (about 15 minutes).

Whirl zucchini mixture, a portion at a time, in a food processor or blender until smooth. Stir in half-and-half, salt, pepper, and ¼ teaspoon of the nutmeg. Cover and refrigerate for at least 4 hours or until next day.

To serve, ladle soup into chilled mugs or bowls and top with additional nutmeg, if desired. Makes about 6 servings.

• GOLDEN YAM SOUP •

An intriguing blend of golden vegetables and Cheddar cheese is the secret to this mellow soup's flavor. Use leftover cooked yams if you have them on hand; if not, bake raw yams in a 400° oven until they're soft when squeezed (45 to 50 minutes). When they're cool enough to handle, peel and mash them.

If you like, serve the hot soup in mugs to sip before a meal, perhaps even a holiday-season dinner.

    3   tablespoons butter or margarine
    1   medium-size onion, chopped
    2   medium-size carrots, cut into ¼-inch-thick
        slices
    1   green bell pepper, seeded and chopped
    2   cups Chicken Stock (page 5) or regular-
        strength canned chicken broth
    ½   teaspoon ground cinnamon
    2   cups cooked, mashed yams
    2   cups milk
    1   cup (4 oz.) shredded sharp Cheddar cheese
    2   tablespoons Worcestershire
        Salt and pepper

In a 4-quart pan, melt butter over medium heat. Add onion, carrots, and bell pepper; cook, stirring occasionally, until onion is soft (about 10 minutes). Stir in stock and cinnamon. Bring to a boil over high heat; reduce heat, cover, and simmer until carrots are very tender when pierced (about 20 minutes). Stir in yams.

Whirl yam mixture, a portion at a time, in a blender until smooth. Return to pan, stir in milk, and heat until steaming. Slowly add cheese and stir constantly until melted. Stir in Worcestershire; season to taste with salt and pepper. Makes about 8 servings.

Bright garden colors offer the promise of fresh vegetable flavor when you serve (clockwise from top) Watercress Soup (facing page), Cauliflower Soup (page 16), Vegetable Soup (page 29), and Tomato Soup (page 27).

LIGHT BUT SATISFYING
S^{OUP}S

PAIR WITH SANDWICH

FIXINGS FOR LUNCH

OR A LIGHT SUPPER

Substantial enough to serve as part of a meal, these soups make excellent menu choices for lunchtime or for those evenings when a lighter-than-usual dinner is called for. To round out the meal, you can offer sandwiches, a selection of cheeses, a platter of cold meats, or whatever else suits your fancy.

The kinds of soup included in the following pages are varied. You'll find a number of chunky vegetable soups, often enriched with cheese, yogurt, or grains. Other choices include a selection of Oriental soups and others fortified with seafood, poultry, or meat.

BEER CHEER CHEESE SOUP

Here's a new twist to the familiar beer-and-pretzel combination: a rich, cheesy soup flavored with Cheddar and beer, and served with pretzels.

- ¼ cup butter or margarine
- ½ cup *each* thinly sliced celery, diced carrot, and chopped onion
- ½ cup all-purpose flour
- ½ teaspoon dry mustard
- ¼ teaspoon thyme leaves
- 4 cups Chicken Stock (page 5) or regular-strength canned chicken broth
- 1½ cups (6 oz.) shredded sharp Cheddar cheese
- 2 tablespoons grated Parmesan cheese
- 1 can (12 oz.) beer
  Salt and pepper
  Pretzels

In a 3-quart pan, melt butter over medium heat. Add celery, carrot, and onion and cook, stirring occasionally, until onion is soft (about 10 minutes).

Stir in flour, mustard, and thyme and cook for 1 minute. Gradually add stock. Bring to a boil over medium-high heat, stirring often; reduce heat, cover, and simmer, stirring occasionally, until vegetables are tender (12 to 15 minutes). Stir in Cheddar and Parmesan cheeses; when melted, add beer. Heat until steaming. Season to taste with salt and pepper. Serve with pretzels. Makes 4 to 6 servings.

LEEK SOUP WITH BRIE

Here's an elegant cousin of French onion soup: set afloat in a leek and mushroom broth are slices of toast topped with melted Brie cheese.

- Dry-toasted French Bread (recipe follows)
- 6 large leeks
- 2 tablespoons butter or margarine
- ½ pound mushrooms, thinly sliced
- 1 clove garlic, minced or pressed
- ½ teaspoon dry tarragon
- ¼ teaspoon white pepper
- 2½ tablespoons all-purpose flour
- 4 cups Chicken Stock (page 5) or regular-strength canned chicken broth
- ⅓ cup whipping cream
- 8 ounces Brie cheese

Prepare Dry-toasted French Bread. Set aside.

Meanwhile, trim and discard ends and tops of leeks, leaving about 3 inches of green leaves. Discard tough outer leaves. Split leeks in half lengthwise; rinse well, then thinly slice.

In a 4 to 5-quart pan, melt butter over medium heat. Add leeks, mushrooms, garlic, tarragon, and pepper. Cook, stirring, until vegetables are very soft and most of the liquid has evaporated (about 15 minutes). Stir in flour; cook until bubbly. Stir in stock and cream, and bring to a boil over medium-high heat, stirring constantly.

Pour soup into ovenproof soup bowls. Top each with a piece of toast, buttered side up. Cut cheese into ½-inch-thick slices, then lay cheese on toast to cover. Place bowls on a rimmed baking sheet and bake in a 425° oven for 10 minutes; then broil about 6 inches below heat until cheese is lightly browned (1 or 2 minutes). Serve at once. Makes 6 servings.

Dry-toasted French Bread. Cut 6 slices **French bread,** each ½ inch thick, to fit inside six 1½ to 2-cup ovenproof soup bowls. Place bread on a baking sheet and bake in a 325° oven until lightly toasted (20 to 25 minutes). Spread each slice with 1 teaspoon **butter** or margarine.

CREAMY LEEK & EDAM SOUP

This country-style soup from Holland is thick with fresh leeks, cooked in a simple milk broth.

- 4 medium-size leeks
- 8 cups Beef Stock (page 5) or regular-strength canned beef broth
- ¾ cup all-purpose flour
- 1 cup milk
- ⅛ teaspoon *each* pepper and ground mace
- ¼ cup whipping cream
- 4 cups (1 lb.) shredded Edam cheese

Trim and discard ends and tops of leeks, leaving about 3 inches of green leaves. Discard tough outer leaves. Split leeks in half lengthwise; rinse well, then thinly slice. Set aside.

In a 5 to 6-quart pan, smoothly blend stock, a little at a time, into flour. Stir in milk, pepper, and mace. Place over medium-high heat and bring to a boil, stirring; reduce heat and simmer for 10 minutes, stirring occasionally. Add leeks and cream; cover and simmer, stirring occasionally, until leeks are tender (about 10 more minutes).

Pass cheese at the table to sprinkle over individual servings. Makes 8 servings.

Crowning each crock of French Onion Soup (facing page) as it emerges
from the oven is a crusty slice of bread topped with cheese. Underneath,
slow-cooked onions flavor the broth for this traditional Gallic treat.

SPINACH & PINE NUT SOUP

Toasted pine nuts add flavor and crunch to this unusual, creamy spinach soup accented with nutmeg.

    1 package (10 oz.) frozen chopped spinach
    4 tablespoons butter or margarine
    ½ cup pine nuts
    1 small onion, chopped
    3 tablespoons all-purpose flour
    ⅛ teaspoon ground nutmeg
    2 cans (10¾ oz. *each*) condensed chicken broth
    2 cups milk

Place spinach in a bowl; let stand at room temperature until thawed.

In a 3 to 4-quart pan, melt 1 tablespoon of the butter over medium heat. Add pine nuts and stir until lightly toasted (3 to 5 minutes). Coarsely chop 3 tablespoons of the nuts, then set all nuts aside in separate bowls.

Melt remaining 3 tablespoons butter in pan. Add onion and cook, stirring occasionally, until soft (about 10 minutes). Stir in the 3 tablespoons chopped nuts, flour, and nutmeg; cook until bubbly. Gradually stir in broth; bring to a boil over medium-high heat, stirring constantly. Add milk and thawed spinach along with any liquid in bowl. Heat, stirring, until steaming.

Pass remaining nuts at the table to spoon over individual servings. Makes 4 to 6 servings.

• FRENCH ONION SOUP •

Pictured on facing page

Under its baked-on topping of toasted bread and melted cheese, this soup has a rich sweetness, accentuated by the addition of port wine. The secret to this version's special flavor is the long, slow cooking of the onions until they caramelize.

    4 tablespoons butter or margarine
    1 tablespoon olive oil or salad oil
    6 large onions, thinly sliced
      Dry-toasted French Bread (page 33)
    6 cups Beef Stock (page 5) or regular-
      strength canned beef broth
      Salt and pepper
    ⅓ cup port
    ½ cup diced Swiss cheese
    ½ cup shredded Swiss cheese
    ½ cup grated Parmesan cheese

In a 4 to 5-quart pan, melt 2 tablespoons of the butter in oil over medium-low heat. Add onions and cook, stirring occasionally, until very soft and caramel-colored but not browned (about 40 minutes). Meanwhile, prepare Dry-toasted French Bread and set aside. Add stock to onions and bring to a boil over high heat; reduce heat, cover, and simmer for 30 minutes. Season to taste with salt and pepper; stir in port.

Pour soup into ovenproof soup bowls. Evenly add the ½ cup diced Swiss cheese and top each serving with a piece of toast, buttered side up. Sprinkle equally with the ½ cup shredded Swiss cheese and then with Parmesan cheese. Melt remaining 2 tablespoons butter and drizzle over.

Place soup bowls on a rimmed baking sheet and bake in a 425° oven for 10 minutes; then broil about 4 inches below heat until cheese is lightly browned (2 minutes). Serve at once. Makes 6 servings.

CREAMY WHITE ONION BISQUE

Whipping cream and white onions make this soup snowy in color and rich in flavor.

    ¼ cup butter or margarine
    6 large white onions, thinly sliced
      Cheesy Toast Rounds (recipe follows)
    2 tablespoons all-purpose flour
    5 cups Chicken Stock (page 5) or regular-
      strength canned chicken broth
    1 cup whipping cream
    ⅛ teaspoon white pepper
      Ground nutmeg

In a 5 to 6-quart pan, melt butter over medium heat. Add onions and cook, stirring often, until very soft (25 to 30 minutes). Meanwhile, toast bread for Cheesy Toast Rounds.

Stir flour into onions; cook until bubbly. Add stock, cream, and pepper. Bring to a boil over medium-high heat, stirring often.

Finish preparing Cheesy Toast Rounds. Ladle soup into 6 bowls; float 2 hot toast rounds in each. Sprinkle with nutmeg. Makes 6 servings.

Cheesy Toast Rounds. Place 12 **baguette slices,** each ½ inch thick, in a single layer on a baking sheet. Bake in a 325° oven until lightly toasted (20 to 25 minutes). Shortly before serving, brush toast rounds with ¼ cup melted **butter** or margarine and sprinkle with ½ cup shredded **Swiss cheese**. Broil about 4 inches below heat until cheese is melted (about 1 minute). Use hot.

TRIPLE GREEN ONION CHOWDER

Three kinds of green onions—leeks, scallions, and chives—go into this delicate, lemon-fragrant soup. Slow cooking brings out their sweetness, while the lemon reinforces their color and enhances their flavor.

6 large leeks
¼ cup butter or margarine
2½ tablespoons all-purpose flour
6 cups Chicken Stock (page 5) or regular-strength canned chicken broth
½ teaspoon thyme leaves
⅛ teaspoon white pepper
3 cups thinly sliced green onions (including tops)
¾ teaspoon grated lemon peel
2 tablespoons lemon juice
½ cup whipping cream, whipped
Whole chives
Thin lemon slices

Trim and discard ends and tops of leeks, leaving about 3 inches of green leaves. Discard tough outer leaves. Split leeks in half lengthwise; rinse well, then thinly slice.

In a 5 to 6-quart pan, melt butter over medium heat. Add leeks and cook, stirring often, until very soft (about 20 minutes). Stir in flour and cook until bubbly. Then gradually add stock and stir in thyme and pepper. Bring to a boil over medium-high heat, stirring constantly. Add onions and cook just until they turn bright green. Stir in lemon peel and lemon juice.

Garnish individual servings with a dollop of whipped cream, some chives, and a lemon slice. Makes about 6 servings.

GAZPACHO IN TOMATO BOWLS

One of the hottest regions of Spain is Andalusia, home of a soup exceptionally well suited to warm weather dining: *gazpacho*. Served icy cold, gazpacho is best described as a cooling tomato salad in soup form.

There are many versions; this one is very chunky and uses large, ripe summer tomatoes hollowed out to serve as soup bowls. (For a heartier version, served with condiments, see Mexican Tomato Gazpacho, this page.)

4 large (3 to 3½-inch diameter) tomatoes
1 medium-size cucumber
1 small red or green bell pepper, seeded and diced
3 green onions (including tops), thinly sliced
2 cloves garlic, minced or pressed
4 teaspoons red wine vinegar
½ teaspoon *each* chili powder and oregano leaves
⅓ cup sour cream
Salt
Liquid hot pepper seasoning

Peel tomatoes, if desired. (To peel, immerse in boiling water to cover for 30 to 40 seconds, then immerse in very cold or ice water until cool; drain and peel.)

Slice tops off tomatoes and reserve. Using a grapefruit knife, hollow out insides, leaving a ¼-inch shell; reserve pulp. Turn shells over on paper towels and let drain.

Lift firm flesh from tomato pulp and dice along with cored tops; place in a bowl. Peel cucumber, cut in half lengthwise, and scoop out and discard seeds. Dice cucumber and add to tomato pulp with bell pepper, onions, garlic, vinegar, chili powder, and oregano. Stir in sour cream, then season to taste with salt and hot pepper seasoning.

Cover and refrigerate soup and tomato shells separately for at least 4 hours or up to 8 hours. To serve, spoon gazpacho into tomato shells; offer remaining soup at the table. Makes 4 servings.

MEXICAN TOMATO GAZPACHO

Embellish this sprightly Mexican gazpacho with your choice of condiments. If you'd prefer a smoother, milder version, try its Salvadorean counterpart, made with cream (facing page).

3½ cups Chicken Stock (page 5) or regular-strength canned chicken broth
2 cans (10 oz. *each*) chili-seasoned tomato cocktail
3 medium-size tomatoes, peeled and chopped
1 tablespoon red wine vinegar
½ teaspoon oregano leaves
1½ tablespoons olive oil or salad oil
Condiments (suggestions follow)

In a large bowl, combine stock, tomato cocktail, tomatoes, vinegar, oregano, and oil. Cover and refrigerate for at least 4 hours or until next day.

Place condiments of your choice in separate bowls. Stir soup well before serving. Pass condiments at the table. Makes 4 to 6 servings.

Condiments. Choose from the following: **Small cooked shrimp;** crumbled crisply cooked **bacon;** pitted, peeled, and chopped **avocado;** seeded, chopped **cucumber;** chopped **green bell pepper;** thinly sliced **green onions** (including tops); **Garlic Seasoned Croutons** (page 21) or purchased seasoned croutons; **lime wedges;** and chopped **fresh cilantro** (coriander).

SALVADOREAN GAZPACHO CREAM

Follow directions for **Mexican Tomato Gazpacho,** but omit tomatoes, vinegar, oregano, and oil; instead, add ½ cup **half-and-half** (light cream).

Omit shrimp, bacon, avocado, lime, and cilantro from condiments; instead, offer shredded **carrot** and seeded, chopped **tomatoes.**

MEXICAN CONDIMENT SOUP

This dish is sure to be a hit at a family supper or informal gathering of any kind. To serve it, you ladle hot soup over avocado slices and shredded cheese; then your offer a selection of cold condiments at the table, so diners can dress up their own servings as they please.

    5 slices bacon
    1 large onion, chopped
    1 clove garlic, minced or pressed
    6 cups Chicken Stock (page 5) or regular-strength canned chicken broth
    1 can (about 1 lb.) tomatoes
    2 medium-size carrots, thinly sliced
    2 medium-size thin-skinned potatoes, peeled and diced
    1 teaspoon sugar
    ½ teaspoon pepper
    Salt
    2 medium-size ripe avocados
    Lemon juice
    2 cups (8 oz.) *each* shredded jack cheese and Cheddar cheese
    Condiments (suggestions follow)

In a 6 to 8-quart pan, cook bacon over medium heat until crisp. Remove from pan, drain, crumble, and set aside to use as a condiment. Discard all but 2 tablespoons of the drippings.

Add onion and garlic to drippings in pan and cook over medium heat, stirring occasionally, until onion is very soft (about 15 minutes). Add stock, tomatoes (break up with a spoon) and their liquid, carrots, potatoes, sugar, and pepper. Bring to a boil over high heat; reduce heat, cover, and simmer until potatoes and carrots are tender (about 25 minutes). Season to taste with salt.

Meanwhile, pit, peel, and thinly slice avocados; lightly coat with lemon juice and set out in a serving bowl. Place cheeses, condiments of your choice, and bacon in separate bowls.

To serve, line soup bowls with cheeses and avocado slices. Ladle hot soup into bowls, then pass condiments at the table. Makes 6 to 8 servings.

Condiments. Choose from the following: **Sour cream,** chopped **green onions** (including tops), chopped **hard-cooked eggs, tortilla chips,** and bottled **green taco sauce.**

AZTEC CORN SOUP

Corn has been basic to Mexican cooking since the days of the Aztecs. Here, it's combined with other favorite Mexican ingredients to produce a creamy south-of-the-border soup. Serve it with warm flour tortillas, if you like.

    ¼ cup butter or margarine
    3½ cups corn cut from cob (5 or 6 medium-size ears)
    1 clove garlic, minced or pressed
    1 cup Chicken Stock (page 5) or regular-strength canned chicken broth
    2 cups milk
    1 teaspoon oregano leaves
    1 can (4 oz.) diced green chilies
    1 cup (4 oz.) shredded jack cheese
    Salt
    1 large tomato, cored and diced
    ¼ cup chopped fresh cilantro (coriander)

In a 5 to 6-quart pan, melt butter over medium heat. Add corn and garlic; cook, stirring, until corn is hot and darker golden in color (about 2 minutes). Remove from heat.

Whirl stock and 2 cups of the corn mixture in a food processor or blender until smooth; add to remaining corn mixture in pan. Stir in milk, oregano, and chilies; bring to a boil over medium heat, stirring constantly. Remove from heat and stir in cheese. Season to taste with salt.

Garnish individual servings with tomato and cilantro. Makes 4 to 6 servings.

CORN CHOWDER

The flavors of corn and bacon complement each other in this simple chowder. A good choice for busy cooks, it uses canned cream-style corn as an easier alternative to cutting kernels from the cob.

  8 slices bacon
  1 large onion, chopped
  4 cups water
  4 cups peeled, diced thin-skinned potatoes
  2 cans (about 1 lb. *each*) cream-style corn
  4 cups milk or 2 cups *each* milk and half-and-half (light cream)
    Salt and seasoned pepper
  2 tablespoons butter or margarine

In a 5-quart pan, cook bacon over medium heat until crisp. Remove from pan, drain, crumble, and set aside; discard all but 2 tablespoons of the drippings.

Add onion to drippings in pan and cook, stirring occasionally, until soft (about 10 minutes). Add water, potatoes, and corn. Bring to a boil over high heat; reduce heat, cover, and simmer until potatoes are tender (about 20 minutes). Stir in milk and season to taste with salt and seasoned pepper. Heat until steaming, then stir in butter.

Pass bacon at the table to sprinkle over individual servings. Makes about 8 servings.

GARDEN CORN SOUP

Fresh corn is joined by a profusion of other vegetables in this chunky soup.

  3 tablespoons butter or margarine
  1 medium-size onion, chopped
  1 clove garlic, minced or pressed
  ½ cup thinly sliced celery
  1 cup shredded carrots
  3½ cups corn cut from cob (5 or 6 medium-size ears)
  2 small thin-skinned potatoes, peeled and diced
  3 medium-size tomatoes, peeled and coarsely chopped
  1 teaspoon *each* sugar and salt
  ¼ teaspoon pepper
  ½ teaspoon dry basil
  3 cups Root Vegetable Stock (page 6) or 3 cups water plus 1 tablespoon instant vegetable bouillon
  1 cup half-and-half (light cream)
    Chopped parsley or thinly sliced green onion (including top)

In a 5-quart pan, melt butter over medium heat. Add onion, garlic, celery, and carrots and cook, stirring occasionally, until vegetables are very soft (about 20 minutes). Add corn, potatoes, tomatoes, sugar, salt, pepper, basil, and stock. Bring to a boil over high heat; reduce heat, cover, and simmer until potatoes are tender (about 20 minutes).

Stir in half-and-half and heat until steaming. Garnish with parsley. Makes about 6 servings.

WINTER MINESTRONE

Pictured on facing page

True to its name, which means "big soup," minestrone is a hearty Italian vegetable soup fortified with pasta. This version is made with winter vegetables and sprinkled with jack cheese.

  3 tablespoons olive oil
  1 large onion, finely chopped
  1 large stalk celery, finely chopped
  2 large cloves garlic, minced or pressed
  1 teaspoon dry basil
  ½ teaspoon *each* dry rosemary, oregano leaves, and thyme leaves
  ¼ cup pearl barley
  2 medium-size thin-skinned potatoes, peeled and diced
  2 large carrots, diced
  8 cups Chicken Stock (page 5) or regular-strength canned chicken broth
  1 large turnip, peeled and diced
  1 can (about 1 lb.) red or white kidney beans (*cannellini*)
  ⅔ cup small shell or elbow macaroni
  ¼ cup tomato paste
  2 cups finely shredded kale leaves or green cabbage
    Salt and pepper
  1½ cups (6 oz.) shredded jack cheese

Heat oil in a 5-quart pan over medium heat. Add onion, celery, garlic, basil, rosemary, oregano, and thyme; cook, stirring occasionally, until onion is soft (about 10 minutes). Add barley, potatoes, carrots, stock, and turnip. Bring to a boil over high heat; reduce heat, cover, and simmer for 20 minutes. Mix in beans and their liquid, macaroni, and tomato paste. Bring to a boil over high heat; reduce heat, cover, and boil gently until macaroni is tender (about 15 minutes). Add kale and cook, uncovered, until kale is tender-crisp (about 5 minutes). Season to taste with salt and pepper.

Pass cheese at the table to sprinkle over individual servings. Makes 8 to 10 servings.

S ay "buon gusto" when you offer bowls of Winter Minestrone (facing page).
Brimming with winter vegetables, beans, and pasta, the lively Italian soup
goes well with the cheese-and-garlic bread called Focaccia (page 59).

GOLDEN TOFU-CAULIFLOWER SOUP

Smooth, golden, and flavored with curry, this zesty Asian-style soup was inspired by a Thai recipe. It contains tofu and cauliflower; spirited seasoning enlivens their subtle flavors.

    2   tablespoons salad oil
    1   medium-size onion, sliced
    2   cloves garlic, minced or pressed
    1   teaspoon curry powder
    2   teaspoons *each* ground coriander and
        ground cumin
    4   cups Chicken Stock (page 5) or regular
        strength canned chicken broth
    2   cups coarsely chopped cauliflower
    ½   pound medium-firm (regular) tofu (bean
        curd), cubed
    1   teaspoon salt
    3   tablespoons lemon juice
    2   tablespoons minced parsley

Heat oil in a 4-quart pan over medium heat. Add onion and cook, stirring occasionally, until soft (about 10 minutes). Stir in garlic, curry powder, coriander, and cumin and cook, stirring, for 1 minute. Add stock, cauliflower, tofu, and salt. Bring to a boil over high heat; reduce heat, cover, and simmer until cauliflower is tender (about 8 minutes).

Whirl cauliflower mixture, a portion at a time, in a food processor or blender until smooth. Return to pan; add lemon juice. Heat, stirring, until steaming. Garnish with parsley. Makes about 4 servings.

VEGETABLE SOUP WITH HERB BUTTER BALLS

Butter balls made with fresh garden herbs season this hot vegetable soup as they melt.

        Herb Butter Balls (recipe follows)
    ½   pound asparagus
    1   medium-size carrot
    2   small thin-skinned potatoes
    5   cups Chicken Stock (page 5) or regular-
        strength canned chicken broth
    1   tablespoon lemon juice
    ⅓   cup thinly sliced green onions (including
        tops)

Prepare Herb Butter Balls and set aside.

Snap off and discard tough ends of asparagus; cut spears into ½-inch slanting slices. Cut carrot

into about ⅓-inch cubes; peel potatoes and cut into ½-inch cubes.

In a 3-quart pan, bring stock and lemon juice to a boil over high heat. Add potatoes; reduce heat, cover, and boil gently for 5 minutes. Add carrot, cover, and cook for 5 more minutes. Add asparagus and onions; cook just until vegetables are tender (about 5 more minutes).

Pass Herb Butter Balls at the table to drop into individual servings. Makes 4 to 6 servings.

Herb Butter Balls. In a small bowl, blend together ¼ cup **butter** (slightly softened) and 2 teaspoons minced **parsley.** Then add one of the following fresh herbs: 1 teaspoon minced **tarragon,** basil, or rosemary; or 2 teaspoons chopped chives. If you don't have fresh herbs, use ½ teaspoon dry tarragon, basil, or rosemary; or 2 teaspoons frozen or freeze-dried chives. Shape mixture into a ball and float in ice water until firm. Cut ball into 16 equal portions. Using chilled wooden butter paddles or your hands, shape portions into balls and chill again in ice water. Serve on ice.

FINNISH SUMMER SOUP

Chunks of tender baby vegetables are featured in this light, creamy soup from Finland.

    2   cups water
    4   to 6 small (1 to 1½-inch diameter) thin-
        skinned potatoes, peeled and halved
    2   tablespoons butter or margarine
    6   small white boiling onions
   12   baby carrots (about ½ lb. *total*) or 1
        package (8 oz.) frozen whole baby carrots
    ½   pound young green beans (ends
        removed), cut into 1-inch lengths, or
        1 package (9 oz.) frozen green beans
    2   cups shelled green peas (about 2 lbs.
        unshelled) or 1 package (10 oz.) frozen
        tiny peas
    2   cups half-and-half (light cream)
    2   tablespoons all-purpose flour
        Salt and pepper

In a 5-quart pan, bring water to a boil over high heat. Add potatoes, butter, onions, and carrots; reduce heat, cover, and boil gently for 8 minutes. Add green beans; cover and boil gently for 8 more minutes. Add peas, and cook until all vegetables are tender when pierced (3 to 5 minutes).

Stir together half-and-half and flour; stir into vegetables. Cook over medium-high heat, stirring, until soup is thickened (3 to 5 minutes). Season to taste with salt and pepper. Makes 4 to 6 servings.

ESCAROLE SOUP

Use the tender inner leaves of a head of escarole (sometimes called broadleaf endive) to make this soup. If you'd like a lighter soup to serve as a first course, just omit the macaroni.

- 1 large head escarole
- ¼ cup small shell or elbow macaroni
  Boiling salted water
- 2 tablespoons butter or margarine
- 2 tablespoons finely chopped onion
- 3½ cups Chicken Stock (page 5) or regular-strength canned chicken broth
- ⅛ teaspoon ground nutmeg
- ¼ teaspoon thyme leaves
  Salt and pepper
  Grated Parmesan cheese

Trim and discard coarse outer leaves of escarole. Stack tender green leaves and slice into strips about ¼ inch wide; set aside. Following package directions, cook macaroni in boiling salted water until tender; drain, rinse under cold water, and drain again.

In a 4 to 5-quart pan, melt butter over medium heat. Add onion and escarole and cook, stirring, for 3 minutes. Stir in stock, nutmeg, and thyme; bring to a boil over high heat. Add cooked macaroni, then season to taste with salt and pepper.

Pass cheese at the table to sprinkle over individual servings. Makes 4 to 6 servings.

ALPHABET VEGETABLE SOUP

Kids will love this colorful alphabet soup, studded with chunks of vegetables as well as alphabet pasta. If you'd like to serve the soup to older diners, you can substitute small soup pasta of another shape.

- 3 tablespoons butter or margarine
- 1 large onion, chopped
- 1 cup *each* diced carrots and peeled, diced thin-skinned potatoes
- ½ cup diced celery
- 1 can (about 1 lb.) tomatoes
- 2 beef bouillon cubes dissolved in 3½ cups boiling water
- ½ teaspoon dry basil
  Salt and pepper
- 3 tablespoons alphabet macaroni
  Boiling salted water

In a 5-quart pan, melt butter over medium heat. Add onion and cook, stirring occasionally, until soft (about 10 minutes). Stir in carrots, potatoes, celery, tomatoes (break up with a spoon) and their liquid, bouillon, and basil. Bring to a boil over high heat; reduce heat, cover, and simmer until vegetables are tender (30 to 35 minutes). Season to taste with salt and pepper.

Meanwhile, following package directions, cook macaroni in boiling salted water until tender; drain, rinse under cold water, and drain again. Add to soup. Makes 4 to 6 servings.

FRESH VEGETABLE-BASIL SOUP

You can vary the fresh vegetables in this soup to suit what's available. To make it heartier, you can add about 2 cups of diced cooked chicken.

- 3 tablespoons butter or margarine
- 1 medium-size onion, chopped
- ½ cup coarsely chopped celery
- 1 medium-size carrot, sliced ⅛ inch thick
- 1 large russet potato
- 2 large tomatoes
- 6 cups Chicken Stock (page 5) or regular-strength canned chicken broth
- ½ teaspoon salt
- ⅛ teaspoon pepper
- 2 tablespoons coarsely chopped fresh basil or 1 teaspoon dry basil
- ½ small head cauliflower, broken into flowerets
- ¼ pound green beans, cut into 2-inch lengths, or 2 small zucchini, sliced ¼ inch thick
- ½ pound green peas, shelled, or 1 cup shredded cabbage
  Grated Parmesan cheese

In a 5 to 6-quart pan, melt butter over medium heat. Add onion, celery, and carrot; cook, stirring occasionally, until vegetables are soft but not browned (about 10 minutes). Meanwhile, peel potato and cut into ½-inch cubes. Also peel and dice tomatoes (you should have about 2 cups). Add potato, tomatoes, stock, salt, pepper, and basil. Bring to a boil over high heat; reduce heat, cover, and simmer for about 20 minutes.

Add cauliflowerets and green beans; simmer for 10 minutes. Add peas, cover, and simmer until all vegetables are tender (about 5 more minutes).

Pass cheese at the table to sprinkle over individual servings. Makes 4 to 6 servings.

Creamy, rich, and satisfying, Shrimp Bisque (facing page) is only one of several flavor variations you can make from our basic potato soup. A pool of melting butter crowns this warming winter dish.

CREAMY POTATO BISQUE

Just by adding or switching a few ingredients, you can turn this creamy potato soup into a fresh mushroom-potato variation or an elegant shrimp, crab, or clam bisque.

6 tablespoons butter or margarine
1 large onion, chopped
1 cup chopped celery (including some leaves)
4 cups peeled, diced thin-skinned potatoes
¼ cup finely chopped parsley
About ½ teaspoon salt
About ¼ teaspoon pepper
4 cups Chicken Stock (page 5) or regular-strength canned chicken broth
4 cups milk
3 tablespoons cornstarch
¼ cup water
Finely chopped parsley

In a 5 to 6-quart pan, melt 4 tablespoons of the butter over medium heat. Add onion and celery and cook, stirring occasionally, until onion is very soft (about 15 minutes). Add potatoes, the ¼ cup parsley, ½ teaspoon of the salt, ¼ teaspoon of the pepper, and stock.

Bring to a boil over high heat; reduce heat, cover, and simmer until potatoes are tender (about 30 minutes).

Stir in milk and heat, covered, until steaming (do not boil). Stir together cornstarch and water and add to soup. Continue cooking and stirring until soup boils and thickens. Season to taste with more salt and pepper, if desired.

Just before serving, pour soup into a tureen, float remaining 2 tablespoons butter on top, and sprinkle with parsley. Makes 6 to 8 servings.

MUSHROOM & POTATO BISQUE

Follow directions for **Creamy Potato Bisque,** but stir in ½ pound sliced **mushrooms** with the stock.

SHRIMP BISQUE

Pictured on facing page

Follow directions for **Creamy Potato Bisque,** but stir in 1¼ pounds **small cooked shrimp** or 2 packages (12 oz. *each*) frozen cooked shrimp, partially thawed, just before adding cornstarch mixture.

CRAB BISQUE

Follow directions for **Creamy Potato Bisque,** adding 1 **bay leaf** with salt and pepper. Stir in 1 pound **crabmeat** just before adding cornstarch mixture.

MINCED CLAM BISQUE

Follow directions for **Creamy Potato Bisque,** but omit the 4 tablespoons butter. Instead, use 5 slices **bacon,** cut into 1-inch pieces. Cook bacon in pan over medium heat until limp (about 5 minutes). Spoon off and discard all but 3 tablespoons of the drippings.

Add onion and celery and cook as directed. Stir in 4 cans (6½ oz. *each*) **minced clams** and their liquid just before adding milk.

BACON VEGETABLE SOUP

Shredded romaine lettuce makes an unusual garnish for this bacon-flavored vegetable soup, adding color, texture, and extra vitamins.

½ pound bacon, chopped
½ pound mushrooms, sliced
1 medium-size onion, chopped
4 cups Chicken Stock (page 5) or regular-strength canned chicken broth
2 medium-size thin-skinned potatoes, peeled and cut into julienne strips
1 large carrot, cut into julienne strips
1 bay leaf
¼ teaspoon ground red pepper (cayenne)
½ cup whipping cream (optional)
1 tablespoon cornstarch (optional)
1½ cups lightly packed shredded romaine lettuce

In a 5 to 6-quart pan, cook bacon over medium heat until crisp. Spoon off and discard all but 2 tablespoons of the drippings. Add mushrooms and onion to drippings in pan; cook, stirring often, until onion is soft and most of the liquid has evaporated (about 10 minutes).

Stir in stock, potatoes, carrot, bay leaf, and red pepper. Stir together cream and cornstarch, if desired, then stir into soup. Bring to a boil over high heat, stirring constantly; reduce heat and simmer, uncovered, stirring occasionally, until carrot and potatoes are tender (about 5 minutes).

Garnish individual servings with romaine. Makes about 4 servings.

PUNJAB PEA SOUP

Though most split pea soups are associated with cold-weather countries, this version is seasoned with curry for an Indian-style flavor variation.

          1 cup dried green split peas
          1 tablespoon salad oil
          1 medium-size onion, thinly sliced
       1½ teaspoons curry powder
          5 cups water
          2 medium-size carrots, sliced
          2 stalks celery, sliced
          1 clove garlic, minced or pressed
          3 chicken bouillon cubes
          1 bay leaf
          1 teaspoon sugar
         ⅛ teaspoon *each* thyme leaves and dry
             rosemary
         ¼ teaspoon pepper
             Salt

Sort split peas to remove debris; rinse well, drain, and set aside.

Heat oil in a 3-quart pan over medium heat. Add onion and curry powder and cook, stirring occasionally, until soft (about 10 minutes). Add water, carrots, celery, split peas, garlic, bouillon cubes, bay leaf, sugar, thyme, rosemary, and pepper. Bring to a boil over high heat; reduce heat, cover, and simmer, stirring occasionally, until peas mash easily (about 1 hour). Remove bay leaf.

Whirl soup, a portion at a time, in a food processor or blender until smooth. Season to taste with salt. Makes 4 to 6 servings.

RED BEAN SOUP

Red beans, bacon, tomato sauce, vinegar, and chili powder—with these ingredients this zesty soup takes on a Southwestern barbecue flavor. You'll need to start soaking the beans the night before you plan to make the soup.

          1 package (12 oz.) dried red beans
          7 cups water
          1 pound slab bacon
          1 large onion, chopped
          1 tablespoon chili powder
         ½ teaspoon *each* pepper and sugar
          2 tablespoons cider vinegar
          3 cans (8 oz. *each*) tomato sauce
          2 cups water

Sort beans to remove debris; rinse well, then drain. Soak overnight in water to cover; drain and rinse. In a 5 to 6-quart pan, bring the 7 cups water to a boil over high heat. Add beans; reduce heat, cover, and boil gently until tender (about 1 hour), adding more water as needed to keep beans covered. Drain well.

Cut off and discard bacon rind; cut bacon into small squares and cook in a wide frying pan over medium heat until browned. Discard all but 2 tablespoons of the drippings, then add onion, chili powder, pepper, and sugar to drippings in pan. Cook, stirring occasionally, until onion is soft (about 10 minutes).

In a 5 to 6-quart pan, combine bacon mixture, beans, vinegar, tomato sauce, and the 2 cups water. Bring to a boil over high heat; reduce heat, cover, and simmer until flavors are well blended (30 to 40 minutes). Makes about 6 servings.

NETHERLANDS BEAN & VEGETABLE SOUP

This simple Dutch soup combines the earthy sweetness of celery root and carrots with tender white beans and bright Brussels sprouts.

          2 tablespoons salad oil
          1 medium-size onion, chopped
         ½ cup all-purpose flour
          6 cups Beef Stock (page 5) or regular-
             strength canned beef broth
          3 cups cooked or 2 cans (about 1 lb. *each*)
             Great Northern beans, drained
          1 medium-size celery root (about 1 lb.),
             peeled and cut into ½-inch cubes
          2 medium-size carrots, thinly sliced
         ¾ pound Brussels sprouts, cut in half
         ½ cup whipping cream

Heat oil in a 6 to 8-quart pan over medium heat. Add onion and cook, stirring occasionally, until soft (about 10 minutes). Stir in flour and cook until bubbly. Gradually stir in stock; add beans, celery root, and carrots. Bring to a boil over high heat, stirring; reduce heat, cover, and simmer for 10 minutes.

Stir in Brussels sprouts and cream and cook, uncovered, just until sprouts are tender (about 10 minutes). Makes about 8 servings.

LEAFY BEAN SOUP

Fresh spinach harmonizes colorfully and deliciously with white kidney beans in this hot soup.

2 tablespoons butter or margarine
1 medium-size onion, finely chopped
1 clove garlic, minced or pressed
3½ cups Chicken Stock (page 5) or regular-
   strength canned chicken broth
1 bay leaf
   About ½ pound spinach
1 can (about 1 lb.) white kidney beans
   (*cannellini*) or garbanzos
   Salt and pepper
   Grated Parmesan cheese

In a 5 to 6-quart pan, melt butter over medium heat. Add onion and garlic and cook, stirring occasionally, until onion is soft (about 10 minutes). Add stock and bay leaf. Bring to a boil over high heat; reduce heat, cover, and simmer for 10 minutes.

Meanwhile, remove and discard tough stems from spinach, then rinse leaves well. Stack leaves and slice into ¼-inch-wide strips; set aside.

Add beans and their liquid to stock. Bring soup back to simmering, then add spinach and cook for 2 minutes. Season to taste with salt and pepper; remove bay leaf. Serve at once.

Pass cheese at the table to sprinkle over individual servings. Makes about 4 servings.

JAMAICAN BLACK BEAN & RICE SOUP

Black beans are well-known in the cooking of the Caribbean and Latin America, where they supply good, earthy flavor to a variety of dishes. The beans are the basis of this distinctive soup from Jamaica; each zesty bowlful is garnished with sliced radishes and green onions, lime juice, and sour cream.

1 pound (about 2½ cups) dried black beans
6 cups water
4 cups Chicken Stock (page 5) or regular-
   strength canned chicken broth
¼ cup olive oil
1 large onion, finely chopped
4 to 6 cloves garlic, minced or pressed
1½ teaspoons *each* ground cumin and oregano
   leaves
   About 2 teaspoons salt
1½ cups cooked rice
   Red wine vinegar
2 cups sour cream
4 green onions (including tops), thinly
   sliced
6 radishes, thinly sliced
   Lime or lemon wedges

Sort beans to remove debris; rinse well, then drain. In a 6 to 8-quart pan, bring beans and water to a boil over high heat. Reduce heat, cover, and simmer until beans swell and absorb most of the water (30 to 45 minutes). Add stock and bring to a boil over high heat; reduce heat, cover, and continue simmering until beans are tender (about 1 more hour).

Meanwhile, heat oil in a wide frying pan over medium heat. Add onion, garlic, cumin, and oregano and cook, stirring occasionally, until onion is soft (about 10 minutes). Set aside.

Whirl about 2 cups of the beans and a small amount of the broth in a food processor or blender until smooth. Return to pan and stir in 2 teaspoons of the salt, onion mixture, and rice; season to taste with vinegar. Heat until steaming. Add more salt, if desired.

Place sour cream, green onions, radishes, and lime wedges in separate bowls and pass at the table to garnish individual servings. Makes 8 to 10 servings.

MUSTARD GREENS & ABALONE SOUP

Pictured on page 47

In Chinese homes, this soup is considered a special-occasion dish. Our recipe calls for canned abalone; if you can't find it, try the chicken variation instead (see page 46).

2 cups mustard greens, cut into 1-inch-wide
   strips, or 2 cups napa or green cabbage,
   cut into 1-inch squares
   Boiling water
1 can (about 8 oz.) abalone
   About 4 cups Chinese Chicken or Pork
   Stock (page 5), Chicken Stock (page 5), or
   regular-strength canned chicken broth
1 teaspoon *each* dry sherry and soy sauce
¼ pound cooked ham, cut into thin slices
   Salt and white pepper

Place mustard greens in boiling water to cover for 1 minute; drain and rinse with cold water. (If using cabbage, do not blanch.)

Drain and measure liquid from abalone. Combine liquid with enough stock to make 5 cups total and pour into a 2-quart pan. Thinly slice abalone and set aside.

Bring stock mixture to a boil over high heat. Add sherry, soy, and mustard greens. Reduce heat and simmer, uncovered, for 3 minutes. Add abalone and ham; heat until steaming. Season to taste with salt and pepper. Makes about 6 servings.

MUSTARD GREENS & CHICKEN SOUP

Follow directions for **Mustard Greens & Abalone Soup** (see page 45), but omit abalone. Increase stock to 5 cups. Skin and bone ½ pound **chicken breast**; cut into bite-size pieces. In a bowl, stir together 1 teaspoon *each* **cornstarch** and **dry sherry**; add chicken and stir to coat. Cook chicken in stock for 5 minutes before adding mustard greens.

CHINESE SHRIMP-TOMATO SOUP

Pictured on facing page

Slivers of thin egg pancake garnish this tomato-flavored soup. The recipe comes from the Shanghai region, in the fertile Yangtse River Valley.

> Egg Slivers (recipe follows)
> ¼ pound **medium-size raw shrimp, shelled and deveined**
> 1 tablespoon **dry sherry**
> ½ small **cucumber**
> 2 tablespoons **salad oil**
> 2 medium-size **tomatoes, peeled, seeded, and coarsely chopped**
> 5 cups **Chinese Chicken or Pork Stock (page 5), Chicken Stock (page 5), or regular-strength canned chicken broth**
> ¼ pound **medium-firm (regular) tofu (bean curd), drained and cut into 1-inch cubes (optional)**
> Salt and white pepper

Prepare Egg Slivers and set aside.

Marinate shrimp in sherry for 10 minutes. Peel cucumber, leaving alternating strips of green for color. Cut in half lengthwise and scoop out seeds; cut crosswise into ¼-inch-thick slices.

Heat oil in a 3-quart pan over medium heat. Add tomatoes and cook, stirring, for 2 minutes. Pour in stock and bring to a boil over high heat. Add shrimp, cucumber, and, if desired, tofu; reduce heat and simmer, uncovered, for 3 minutes. Season to taste with salt and pepper.

Garnish individual servings with Egg Slivers. Makes 4 to 6 servings.

Egg Slivers. In a small bowl, beat 2 **eggs** with 2 teaspoons **water** and ⅛ teaspoon **salt.** Heat 2 teaspoons **salad oil** in a wide frying pan over medium heat. Pour in egg mixture and tilt pan to distribute evenly. Cook until egg is set but still moist. Turn out and let cool. Roll loosely, then cut roll crosswise into slivers.

WON TON SOUP

Even a novice can easily duplicate a professional-looking Chinese won ton soup. You start with purchased won ton skins (look in your market's refrigerator or freezer section). The skins are sold in 1-pound packages, each containing 70 to 80 sheets of the paper-thin squares.

We've found it most efficient to use the whole package of skins at one time, then freeze some of the won ton to make more soup another time.

> 36 **Pork-filled Won Ton (recipe follows), thawed if frozen**
> 6 cups **Chinese Chicken or Pork Stock (page 5), Chicken Stock (page 5), or regular-strength canned chicken broth**
> 2 cups thickly sliced **napa cabbage or bok choy**
> 3 **green onions (including tops), thinly sliced**
> 1 teaspoon *each* **soy sauce and sugar**
> ½ teaspoon **sesame oil**
> Chopped fresh **cilantro (coriander)**

Prepare Pork-filled Won Ton. Bring a large pan of water to a boil over high heat. Drop in won ton; reduce heat and simmer, uncovered, until pork in filling is no longer pink (about 4 minutes). Drain well.

Meanwhile, pour stock into a 3 to 4-quart pan and bring to a boil over medium-high heat. Add cabbage and onions and cook for 3 minutes. With a slotted spoon, remove won ton from water and drop into hot stock. Add soy, sugar, and oil. Garnish with cilantro. Makes 6 servings.

Pork-filled Won Ton. In a bowl, combine 1 pound **lean ground pork** (or ½ pound *each* lean ground pork and medium-size raw shrimp, shelled, deveined, and finely chopped); ⅓ cup **water chestnuts,** finely chopped; 2 **green onions** (including tops), finely chopped; 1 tablespoon **soy sauce;** ½ teaspoon **salt;** ⅛ teaspoon **pepper;** ½ teaspoon minced **fresh ginger;** and 2 teaspoons **dry sherry;** stir until blended. In a bowl, beat 1 **egg** lightly.

Unwrap 1 package (1 lb.) **won ton skins;** cover with a damp towel to keep pliable. Place 1 won ton skin on a flat surface. Mound 1 teaspoon of the pork filling in a corner; then fold that corner over, tucking point under. Moisten corners on either side of filling with beaten egg; bring together behind filled corner, overlapping slightly. Pinch together firmly. Repeat with remaining skins, placing filled won ton slightly apart on a baking sheet; cover. If not using immediately, refrigerate for up to 8 hours; or freeze until firm, then transfer to plastic bags and return to freezer. Thaw, covered, in a single layer. Makes 70 to 80.

voke the magic of the Orient with these four Chinese soups. Clockwise from
top: Shrimp Ball Soup (page 51), Mustard Greens & Abalone Soup (page 45),
Chinese Shrimp-Tomato Soup (facing page), and Hot & Sour Soup (page 48).

HOT & SOUR SOUP

A classic on Chinese restaurant menus, this warming soup is not difficult to prepare at home.

    4   medium-size Oriental dried mushrooms
    ¼   pound lean boneless pork, cut into
        matchstick pieces
    1   tablespoon dry sherry
    4   cups Chinese Chicken or Pork Stock (page
        5), Chicken Stock (page 5), or regular-
        strength canned chicken broth
    ½   pound chicken breast, skinned, boned,
        and cut into matchstick pieces
    ½   cup sliced bamboo shoots, cut into
        matchstick pieces
    ¼   pound medium-firm (regular) tofu (bean
        curd), drained and cut into ½-inch cubes
    2   tablespoons white wine vinegar
    1   tablespoon soy sauce
    2   tablespoons cornstarch
    ¼   cup water
    ½   to ¾ teaspoon white pepper
    1   teaspoon sesame oil
    1   egg
        Salt
    2   green onions (including tops), cut into 1-
        inch slanting slices

Soak mushrooms in warm water to cover for 30 minutes; drain. Cut off and discard stems; squeeze caps dry and thinly slice. Combine pork with sherry; let stand for 10 minutes.

In a 3-quart pan, bring stock to a boil over high heat. Add mushrooms, pork, chicken, and bamboo shoots. Stir several times; reduce heat, cover, and simmer for 5 minutes. Add tofu, vinegar, and soy; simmer, uncovered, for 1 more minute.

Stir together cornstarch and water; add to stock mixture and cook, stirring, until slightly thickened. Remove from heat. Add pepper and oil. Lightly beat egg; slowly pour into soup, stirring constantly. Season to taste with salt.

Garnish individual servings with onion slices. Makes about 6 servings.

YOGURT SOUP WITH BARLEY & SPINACH

This nourishing hot soup is made with yogurt and topped with a flavorful mint-onion butter. Since the yogurt is stabilized with cornstarch, the soup can be boiled without curdling—and it reheats well.

    7   to 8 cups Chicken Stock (page 5) or
        regular-strength canned chicken broth
    ½   cup pearl barley
        About 1 pound spinach or 1 package
        (10 oz.) frozen leaf spinach
    3   tablespoons *each* cornstarch and water
    2   cups plain yogurt
    2   teaspoons sugar
    ¼   cup butter or margarine
    1   medium-size onion, chopped
    2   cloves garlic, minced or pressed
    2   tablespoons finely chopped fresh mint or
        4 teaspoons crushed dry mint leaves
        Salt and pepper

In a 3 to 4-quart pan, bring 7 cups of the stock to a boil over high heat. Add barley; reduce heat, cover, and simmer until tender (about 1 hour).

Meanwhile, remove and discard tough stems from spinach, then rinse leaves well. Stack leaves and slice crosswise into ½-inch-wide strips. (Or partially thaw frozen spinach and cut into strips; thaw completely and drain well.) Set aside.

In a small pan, blend cornstarch and water over medium-low heat until smooth, then stir in yogurt and sugar. Bring to a boil, stirring often. Remove from heat and let cool.

In a small frying pan, melt butter over medium heat. Add onion and garlic and cook, stirring occasionally, until onion is soft (about 10 minutes). Stir in mint. Remove from heat and set aside.

Add spinach to stock mixture and simmer for 3 minutes. Stir in yogurt mixture, bring to a boil over medium-high heat, and cook, stirring, for 3 more minutes. Thin soup with additional stock, if desired. Season to taste with salt and pepper.

Serve in a tureen, spooning onion mixture over top. Makes 6 to 8 servings.

CREAMY LENTIL SOUP

This Lebanese soup uses red lentils, a Middle Eastern variety available in markets that carry imported foods. If you can't find red lentils, use brown ones.

    1   cup Garlic Seasoned Croutons (page 21) or
        2 tablespoons butter or margarine plus 1
        cup purchased seasoned croutons
    1   cup red lentils
    4   cups water
    1   large russet potato, peeled and diced
    2   tablespoons butter or margarine
    1   small onion, finely chopped
    2   *each* beef and chicken bouillon cubes
    ½   cup half-and-half (light cream) or milk
        Salt and pepper

Prepare Garlic Seasoned Croutons. (Or melt butter in a small frying pan over medium heat; add purchased croutons and cook, stirring often, until lightly toasted.) Set aside.

Sort lentils to remove debris; rinse well, then drain. In a 3-quart pan, bring lentils and water to a boil over high heat. Add potato; reduce heat, cover, and simmer until lentils and potato mash easily (about 45 minutes).

Meanwhile, in a small frying pan, melt butter over medium-low heat. Add onion and cook, stirring occasionally, until golden brown (about 15 minutes). Add to lentils along with bouillon cubes, stirring to dissolve cubes.

Whirl lentil mixture, a portion at a time, in a food processor or blender until smooth. Return to pan and add half-and-half; thin with a little water if needed. Season to taste with salt and pepper; heat until steaming.

Pass croutons at the table to sprinkle over individual servings. Makes about 4 servings.

LENTIL SOUP WITH LEMON

Considering all the nourishment they provide, lentils are one of today's best food buys. Like dry beans, they're rich in vegetable protein, iron, minerals, and especially the B vitamins. But lentils cook more quickly than beans and don't require soaking. Try cooking them with Swiss chard and potatoes in this savory soup accented with lemon.

About 1½ pounds Swiss chard
1 bunch fresh cilantro (coriander)
1½ cups lentils
7 to 8 cups water
4 beef bouillon cubes
6 tablespoons olive oil or salad oil
1 medium-size onion, finely chopped
3 cloves garlic, minced or pressed
1 medium-size thin-skinned potato, peeled and diced
¾ teaspoon salt
¼ teaspoon pepper
½ teaspoon ground cumin
3 tablespoons lemon juice
Thin lemon slices

Rinse and drain chard; cut off and discard thickest part of white stems, then stack leaves and cut crosswise into ½-inch-wide strips. Set aside.

Coarsely chop a quarter of the cilantro; set aside. Finely chop remaining cilantro and set aside.

Sort lentils to remove debris; rinse well, then drain. In a 5-quart pan, bring lentils, 7 cups of the water, and bouillon cubes to a boil over high heat. Reduce heat, cover, and simmer for 20 minutes.

Meanwhile, heat oil in a small frying pan over medium-low heat. Add onion and garlic; cook, stirring occasionally, until soft and golden (15 to 20 minutes), adding finely chopped cilantro during last few minutes of cooking. Set aside.

Add potato to lentil mixture and simmer for 15 minutes; then stir in onion mixture and chard and continue simmering until vegetables and lentils are tender to bite (about 5 more minutes). Stir in salt, pepper, cumin, and lemon juice. If desired, thin soup with up to 1 cup more water.

Top individual servings with coarsely chopped cilantro and lemon slices. Makes 6 servings.

BULGUR VEGETABLE SOUP

Combining short-cut ingredients with fresh foods and seasonings you probably keep on hand is a great way to make homemade soup in a hurry.

3 slices bacon
1 large onion, chopped
1 clove garlic, minced or pressed
3½ cups Beef Stock (page 5) or regular-strength canned beef broth
1 can (8 oz.) tomato sauce
½ green bell pepper, chopped
1 stalk celery, thinly sliced
⅓ cup bulgur wheat
½ teaspoon Italian herb seasoning or ⅛ teaspoon *each* dry basil and oregano, thyme, and marjoram leaves
1 package (10 oz.) frozen mixed vegetables
Salt and pepper
Chopped parsley

In a 5 to 6-quart pan, cook bacon over medium heat until crisp. Remove from pan, drain, crumble, and set aside; discard all but 1 tablespoon of drippings.

Add onion and garlic to drippings in pan and cook, stirring occasionally, until onion is soft (about 10 minutes). Add stock, tomato sauce, bell pepper, celery, bulgur, and herb seasoning. Bring to a boil over high heat; reduce heat, cover, and simmer for about 25 minutes. Add frozen vegetables and cook until tender (about 8 minutes). Season to taste with salt and pepper.

Top individual servings with bacon and parsley. Makes 4 to 6 servings.

• OYSTER STEW •

Many people who shun uncooked oysters are enthusiastic about the flavor that pervades a good oyster stew. Here's a rich, creamy version that is simple to prepare and will win the hearts of everyone.

  6 **slices bacon, diced**
  1 **clove garlic, minced or pressed**
3½ **cups Fish Stock (page 6), Chicken Stock (page 5), or regular-strength canned chicken broth**
  2 **jars (10 oz. *each*) small Pacific oysters**
  4 **cups whipping cream**
  ¼ **cup *each* chopped parsley and grated Parmesan cheese**
      About 2 tablespoons butter or margarine
      Dill weed (optional)

In a 3 to 4-quart pan, cook bacon over medium heat until crisp. Remove from pan, drain, and set aside; discard all but 1 teaspoon of the drippings. Add garlic to drippings in pan and cook, stirring, for 1 minute.

Pour in stock and oysters (cut larger oysters in half) and their liquid. Bring to a simmering over medium-high heat. When oysters begin to plump, stir in cream; heat until steaming.

Garnish individual servings with parsley, cheese, about a teaspoon of the butter, dill weed, if desired, and bacon. Makes about 6 servings.

• CHILI CLAM CHOWDER •

Red clam chowder isn't usually made with Mexican-style seasonings, but they do add interesting flavor and lift the soup out of the ordinary. To carry out the Mexican theme, serve it with *quesadillas*—folded flour tortillas with jack cheese melted inside.

  1 **tablespoon olive oil or salad oil**
  1 **medium-size onion, chopped**
  1 **small clove garlic, minced or pressed**
  1 **tablespoon all-purpose flour**
  1 **large can (1 lb. 12 oz.) tomatoes, whirled in a food processor or blender until smooth**
  3 **cans (6½ oz. *each*) chopped clams**
  2 **teaspoons sugar**
  2 to 3 **teaspoons chili powder**
  ½ **teaspoon thyme leaves**
  2 **cups peeled, diced thin-skinned potatoes**
  ½ **cup finely chopped green bell pepper**
      Salt and pepper

Heat oil in a 5 to 6-quart pan over medium heat. Add onion and cook, stirring occasionally, until soft (about 10 minutes). Add garlic and flour; cook, stirring, until bubbly. Gradually stir in tomatoes. Drain liquid from clams and add to soup, reserving clams. Stir in sugar, chili powder, thyme, potatoes, and bell pepper. Bring to a boil over high heat; reduce heat, cover, and simmer until potatoes are tender when pierced (about 20 minutes).

Add clams and heat until steaming. Season to taste with salt and pepper. Makes 4 to 6 servings.

• CREAMY CLAM CHOWDER •

New Englanders are partial to a thick, creamy soup made from clams, bacon, cream, and potatoes. Known as chowder, it gets its name from the French *chaudière*, meaning "kettle."

This version adds a few extra ingredients and plenty of savory seasonings for a distinctive and tasty result.

  6 **slices bacon, diced**
  2 **medium-size carrots, thinly sliced**
  2 **stalks celery, thinly sliced**
  1 **small onion, chopped**
  ½ **small green bell pepper, chopped**
  1 **clove garlic, minced or pressed**
1½ **pounds thin-skinned potatoes**
  2 **bottles (8 oz. *each*) clam juice**
  8 **cans (6½ oz. *each*) chopped clams**
  1 **bay leaf**
  ½ **teaspoon liquid hot pepper seasoning**
  ¼ **teaspoon pepper**
1½ **teaspoons Worcestershire**
  ¾ **teaspoon thyme leaves**
  4 **cups whipping cream**
      Salt

In a 6 to 8-quart pan, cook bacon over medium heat until crisp. Remove from pan, drain, and set aside; discard all but 2 tablespoons of the drippings. Add carrots, celery, onion, bell pepper, and garlic to drippings in pan and cook, stirring often, until onion is soft (about 10 minutes).

Cut potatoes into ½-inch cubes. Add to vegetable mixture along with clam juice. Bring to a boil; reduce heat, cover, and simmer until potatoes are tender when pierced (about 15 minutes). Stir in clams and their liquid, bay leaf, hot pepper seasoning, pepper, Worcestershire, thyme, cream, and bacon. Heat until steaming; season to taste with salt. Makes 8 to 10 servings.

CHILLED SEAFOOD POTPOURRI

This unusual warm-weather soup is made with buttermilk, which adds nourishment as well as an interesting piquant flavor. But its presence isn't obvious, so the soup pleases even those who don't ordinarily like buttermilk.

Since the ingredients aren't cooked together, ample time must be allowed for their flavors to blend during chilling.

> 2 green onions (including tops), thinly sliced
> 2 tablespoons minced green bell pepper
> 1 cup peeled, diced cucumber
> 1 teaspoon *each* dry tarragon, salt, and Dijon mustard
> 2¼ teaspoons sugar
> 2 teaspoons Worcestershire
> Dash of liquid hot pepper seasoning
> 6 cups buttermilk
> ⅔ cup milk
> About 1 cup crabmeat
> About 1½ cups small cooked shrimp

In a large bowl, stir together onions (reserve some green tops for garnish), bell pepper, cucumber, tarragon, salt, mustard, sugar, Worcestershire, and hot pepper seasoning; stir in buttermilk and milk. Flake crabmeat; cut shrimp into bite-size pieces if large. Stir shellfish into soup. Cover and refrigerate until well chilled.

Just before serving, stir well and garnish with reserved onion tops. Makes about 6 servings.

SHRIMP BALL SOUP

Pictured on page 47

Bright pea pods, cilantro sprigs, fluffy shrimp balls, and mushrooms all float in this picture-pretty soup.

> Shrimp Balls (recipe follows)
> 2 ounces bean threads
> 4 cups Chinese Chicken or Pork Stock (page 5), Chicken Stock (page 5), or regular-strength canned chicken broth
> 1 teaspoon *each* dry sherry and soy sauce
> ¼ pound mushrooms, thinly sliced
> 20 Chinese pea pods (also called snow or sugar peas), ends and strings removed
> Salt
> Fresh cilantro (coriander) sprigs

Prepare Shrimp Balls; set aside.

Soak bean threads in warm water to cover for 30 minutes. Drain; cut into 6-inch lengths.

In a 2-quart pan, bring stock, sherry, and soy to a boil over high heat. Add bean threads and mushrooms; reduce heat and simmer, uncovered, for 5 minutes. Add pea pods and cook for 2 more minutes. Add shrimp balls and cook just until heated through. Season to taste with salt. Garnish with cilantro. Makes 4 to 6 servings.

Shrimp Balls. In a bowl, beat 1 **egg white** until foamy. In another bowl, stir together 2 teaspoons *each* **dry sherry** and **cornstarch**; add to egg white along with ½ teaspoon *each* **salt** and grated **fresh ginger**. Mix in ¼ cup **water chestnuts,** finely chopped, and ½ pound medium-size **raw shrimp,** shelled, deveined, and finely chopped. Coat hands with **salad oil;** roll shrimp mixture into walnut-size balls. Heat a 2 to 3-quart pan of **water** to simmering. Drop in balls, a few at a time, and simmer until they float (4 to 5 minutes); lift out.

QUICK CRAB CHOWDER

Fresh, frozen, or canned crabmeat can be used to make this sherry-seasoned soup. It makes a nice change from clam chowder when you're in the mood for something different.

> 3 slices bacon, diced
> 1 large onion, finely chopped
> 1 tablespoon all-purpose flour
> 3 medium-size thin-skinned potatoes, cooked, peeled, and diced, or 1 can (about 1 lb.) whole new potatoes, drained and diced
> 3 cups milk
> Salt and pepper
> 1½ cups fresh or thawed frozen crabmeat or 2 cans (about 7 oz. *each*) crabmeat, drained
> ¼ cup finely chopped parsley
> 1 tablespoon dry sherry

In a 3 to 4-quart pan, cook bacon over medium heat until crisp. Remove from pan, drain, and set aside; reserve drippings. Add onion to drippings in pan and cook, stirring occasionally, until soft (about 10 minutes). Stir in flour and potatoes and cook, stirring, for 1 minute. Remove from heat and gradually stir in milk; return to heat and cook, stirring, until bubbly and slightly thickened.

Season to taste with salt and pepper. Stir in crabmeat, parsley, sherry, and bacon. Heat until steaming; serve immediately. Makes about 4 servings.

SOUPS FROM THE MICROWAVE

With a microwave oven, it takes just minutes to make a sturdy whole-meal soup with flavor and aroma as tantalizing as those of a soup that simmers for hours. Or on warm days, you can turn out refreshing cold soups.

Below you'll find examples of these and other kinds of soups you can make in the microwave; be sure to prepare them only in utensils that are recommended for microwave ovens, such as glass or ceramic dishes. For our testing, we used 650-watt microwave ovens.

CREAMY BEET SOUP

- 6 cups peeled, diced beets (about 7 medium-size)
- 3½ cups Chicken Stock (page 5) or regular-strength canned chicken broth
- 2 cups buttermilk
- 1 teaspoon dill weed
  Salt and pepper
- ¾ cup thinly sliced green onions (including tops)
- 1 large apple
- 2 teaspoons lemon juice
  Sour cream

In a 3-quart baking dish, combine beets and ½ cup of the stock. Cover and cook on **HIGH (100%)** for 20 minutes or until tender, stirring several times. Add the remaining 3 cups stock.

Whirl beet mixture, a portion at a time, in a food processor or blender until smooth. Stir in buttermilk and dill weed, and season to taste with salt and pepper. Add onions. Cover and refrigerate until well chilled. Core and dice apple; add lemon juice and mix well. Pass apple and sour cream at the table to spoon over individual servings. Makes 8 to 10 servings.

COOL GOLDEN CHOWDER

- 2 tablespoons butter or margarine
- 1 medium-size onion, chopped
- 1 cup chopped carrots
- 2½ cups chopped crookneck squash
- 2 cups Chicken Stock (page 5) or regular-strength canned chicken broth
- 1 cup corn cut from cob (about 2 medium-size ears)
- ¼ teaspoon thyme leaves
  Salt and pepper
- ½ cup milk
  Chopped parsley
  Salted sunflower seeds

In a 2 or 2½-quart baking dish, cook butter, uncovered, on **HIGH (100°)** for 30 seconds. Add onion, cover, and cook for 2 minutes. Stir in carrots, squash, and ½ cup of the stock; cover and cook for 5 minutes. Add corn; cover and cook for 8 minutes or until vegetables are tender to bite. Add remaining 1½ cups stock.

Whirl vegetable mixture, a portion at a time, in a food processor or blender until smooth. Add thyme and season to taste with salt and pepper. Cover and refrigerate until well chilled. Stir in milk.

Garnish with parsley and sunflower seeds. Makes 4 to 6 servings.

GREEN BEAN BISQUE

- ⅓ cup slivered almonds
- 2 tablespoons butter or margarine
- 1 clove garlic, minced or pressed
- 1 medium-size onion, chopped
- 4 cups green beans, cut into 1-inch pieces
- 3½ cups Chicken Stock (page 5) or regular-strength canned chicken broth
- ¼ teaspoon savory leaves
  Salt and pepper
  Sour cream

In a bowl, cook almonds, uncovered, on **HIGH (100%)** until golden, stirring once or twice; set aside.

In a 2-quart casserole, cook butter, uncovered, for 30 seconds. Add garlic and onion; cover and cook for 2 minutes. Stir in beans and ½ cup of the stock. Cover and cook for 10 minutes or until beans are tender. Add remaining 3 cups stock.

Whirl vegetable mixture, a portion at a time, in a food processor or blender until smooth. Add savory and season to taste with salt and pepper. Cover and refrigerate until well chilled.

Garnish individual servings with a dollop of sour cream and toasted almonds. Makes 4 to 6 servings.

SWEET-SOUR BEAN SOUP

8 slices bacon, diced
1 small onion, chopped
1 clove garlic, minced or pressed
1 can (about 1 lb.) stewed tomatoes
2 cans (about 1 lb. *each*) red kidney beans
1 teaspoon chili powder
¼ teaspoon *each* thyme leaves and dry basil
2 tablespoons red wine vinegar
Sour cream (optional)

Separate bacon pieces and spread over bottom of a 3-quart casserole or soup tureen. Cover and cook on **HIGH (100%)** for 5 minutes, stirring after 3 minutes. With a slotted spoon, lift out bacon, drain, and set aside; discard all but 2 tablespoons of the drippings.

Add onion and garlic to drippings in casserole. Cover and cook for 4 minutes, stirring after 2 minutes. Add tomatoes (break up with a spoon) and their liquid. Reserve 1 cup of the beans; place remaining beans and their liquid in casserole. Mash reserved beans with a fork and add to casserole along with chili powder, thyme, and basil. Stir until ingredients are well combined. Cover and cook until steaming (8 to

10 minutes) stirring after 4 minutes. Stir in vinegar and bacon.

If desired, pass sour cream at the table to spoon over individual servings. Makes 4 to 6 servings.

SAUSAGE SOUP OLÉ

1 pound bulk pork sausage
1½ cups thinly sliced carrots
1 envelope dry onion soup mix (enough for 4 to 6 servings)
5 cups hot water
1 can (about 1 lb.) small whole onions, drained
1 can (about 1 lb.) red kidney beans, drained
1 can (about 1 lb.) stewed tomatoes
1 can (about 1 lb.) baby corn, drained
1 teaspoon oregano leaves
½ teaspoon ground cumin
Condiments (suggestions follow)
Cilantro (coriander) sprigs (optional)

Crumble sausage into a deep 4 to 5-quart casserole or soup tureen. Cover and cook on **HIGH (100%)** for 6 minutes, stirring every 2 minutes. Drain off and discard all fat. Stir in carrots, onion soup mix, and 1 cup of the water. Cover and cook until carrots are tender when pierced (8 to 10 minutes), stirring once or twice.

Add onions, beans, tomatoes (break up with a spoon) and their liquid, corn, oregano, cumin, and remaining 4 cups water. Cover and cook until steaming (about 8 minutes), stirring several times.

Place condiments of your choice in separate bowls to pass at the table. Before serving, garnish soup with cilantro, if desired. Makes about 8 servings.

Condiments. Choose from the following: Sliced **green onions** (including tops), **sour cream, avocado cubes, green chile salsa** or taco sauce, and **lime wedges.**

SPICED TOMATO SEAFOOD SOUP

Take your choice of seafood for this zesty tomato soup—you can offer just one kind or a variety. If you put out several kinds, you can let your guests help themselves to a bowlful of broth directly from the pan, then add the shellfish they prefer.

>   2 tablespoons butter or margarine
>   1 large onion, chopped
>   1 teaspoon thyme leaves
>   3 tablespoons Worcestershire
> 12 cups Fish Stock (page 6), Chicken Stock (page 5), or regular-strength canned chicken broth
>   4 cups chili-seasoned tomato cocktail
>   1 to 1½ pounds cooked shellfish, such as small shrimp, crabmeat, or diced lobster

In a 5 to 6-quart pan, melt butter over medium heat. Add onion and cook, stirring occasionally, until soft (about 10 minutes). Stir in thyme, Worcestershire, stock, and tomato cocktail. Bring to a boil over high heat; reduce heat, cover, and simmer for 5 minutes.

Place shellfish near soup. Let guests serve themselves, adding shellfish of their choice to each bowl of soup. Makes about 8 servings.

DUTCH SHRIMP SOUP

Delicately seasoned with dill and paprika, this creamy tomato broth is enlivened by the last-minute addition of tiny pink shrimp and lemon juice.

>   ¼ cup butter or margarine
>   5 tablespoons all-purpose flour
>   2 cups Fish Stock (page 6), Chicken Stock (page 5), or regular-strength canned chicken broth
>   3 cups milk
>   ¼ cup whipping cream
>   ¼ cup finely chopped parsley
>   1 teaspoon *each* paprika and dill weed
>   5 tablespoons tomato paste
>   3 tablespoons lemon juice
>   1 pound small cooked shrimp
>   Pepper

In a 3 to 4-quart pan, melt butter over medium-high heat. Add flour and cook, stirring, until bubbly. Remove from heat and gradually stir in stock. Return to heat and cook, stirring, until thickened.

Gradually stir in milk and cream; then stir in

parsley, paprika, dill weed, and tomato paste. Heat until steaming. Stir in lemon juice and shrimp and cook for 1 minute. Season to taste with pepper. Makes about 6 servings.

MATZO BALL SOUP

The pride of a traditional Jewish cook, matzo balls are tender, fluffy dumplings served in chicken soup for Passover and other holiday meals. Matzo meal is the ingredient that distinguishes them from other dumplings; it absorbs moisture readily, retaining a light, porous texture. Look for matzo meal in the Jewish foods section of a well-stocked market.

To make matzo balls, the dough must be refrigerated, so mix it ahead of time. Don't be concerned that it's still sticky when you form the balls.

>   3 eggs
>   3 tablespoons water
>   2 tablespoons finely chopped onion
>   3 tablespoons chicken fat or solid vegetable shortening, melted and cooled
> 1¼ teaspoons salt
>   ⅛ teaspoon *each* ground nutmeg and pepper
>   ⅓ cup chopped parsley
>   ¾ cup matzo meal
>   6 cups Chicken Stock (page 5) or regular-strength canned chicken broth
>   2 medium-size carrots, thinly sliced

In a large bowl, lightly beat eggs; then stir in water, onion, chicken fat, salt, nutmeg, pepper, and 3 tablespoons of the parsley. Add matzo meal and stir until blended. Cover and refrigerate for 30 minutes. With your hands, shape rounded tablespoons of the matzo mixture into balls (it will be slightly sticky).

In a 2 to 3-quart pan, bring stock to a boil over high heat. Add carrots and matzo balls; reduce heat, cover, and simmer until matzo balls are firm to touch and a wooden pick inserted in center comes out clean (about 35 minutes).

Before serving, sprinkle soup with remaining parsley. Makes 4 to 6 servings.

CREAMY CHICKEN SOUP

Introducing a surprise ingredient or two can often elevate familiar foods to memorable dishes. For instance, coconut, curry, and yogurt give a lively new dimension to this chicken soup.

Chicken and Stock (recipe follows)
2 cups milk
⅓ cup flaked or shredded sweetened coconut
2 strips lemon peel (¼ by 2 inches *each*)
¼ cup butter or margarine
¼ cup all-purpose flour
1 teaspoon curry powder
½ cup plain yogurt
Salt and pepper
About ⅓ cup *each* slivered almonds and sliced green onions (including tops)

Prepare Chicken and Stock; set each aside.

In a small pan, scald milk; remove from heat, add coconut and lemon peel, and let cool completely. Pour through a wire strainer and discard coconut and peel.

In a 3-quart pan, melt butter over medium heat. Stir in flour and curry powder and cook until bubbly; gradually add stock and cook, stirring, until thickened. With a wire whisk, blend in coconut-seasoned milk, yogurt, and chicken. Season to taste with salt and pepper. Heat until steaming.

Pass almonds and onions at the table to sprinkle over individual servings. Makes 6 servings.

Chicken and Stock. In a 3-quart pan, place a 1-pound **chicken breast,** split; 1 cup **celery leaves;** 1 large **onion,** sliced; 4 **whole cloves;** and 3 cups **Chicken Stock** (page 5) or regular-strength canned chicken broth. Bring to a boil over high heat; reduce heat, cover, and simmer for 1 hour. Lift out chicken and let cool. Meanwhile, pour stock through a wire strainer set over a bowl; discard seasonings and vegetables and reserve stock.

Discard bones and skin from cooled chicken; tear meat into bite-size pieces.

• TURKEY SOUP •

Not a thing is wasted when you make this simple and delicious soup from leftover roast turkey—the bones flavor the broth, the meat adds substance and texture. The soup is an ideal choice for a post-holiday lunch.

1 roasted turkey carcass, with some meat attached
10 cups water
About 1 teaspoon salt
About ¼ teaspoon pepper
1 medium-size onion, sliced
1 medium-size carrot, sliced
5 cups finely shredded napa cabbage
Chopped parsley

Strip carcass of any large pieces of meat; dice enough meat to make 2 cups and set aside.

In a 5 to 6-quart pan, combine turkey carcass, water, 1 teaspoon of the salt, ¼ teaspoon of the pepper, onion, and carrot. Bring to a boil over high heat; reduce heat, cover, and simmer for 2 hours. Let cool slightly, then pour through a wire strainer. Remove any remaining meat from bones and stir into broth along with diced turkey meat; discard vegetables and bones.

Heat broth to boiling. Add cabbage; reduce heat, cover, and simmer for 10 minutes. Season to taste with more salt and pepper. Garnish with parsley. Makes about 8 servings.

• KOHLRABI CHICKEN SOUP •

Kohlrabi is a curious-looking vegetable with a delicate, turniplike flavor (in German, *kohl* means cabbage and *rabi* means turnip). Kohlrabi looks like a root vegetable, but the bulb-shaped section is actually the stem—the base of the plant's leaf stalks—that forms above ground. Leaves and stems are both good to eat.

Kohlrabi is available almost year round and is usually sold in bunches of three or four bulbs. When combined with chicken and seasoned lightly with nutmeg, it makes a delicious, low-calorie soup.

6 to 8 small or medium-size kohlrabi
3 tablespoons butter or margarine
1 large onion, chopped
6 cups Chicken Stock (page 5) or regular-strength canned chicken broth
⅛ teaspoon ground nutmeg
2 cups cubed cooked chicken
Salt and pepper

Cut leaves and stems from kohlrabi, discarding tough leaves and stems. Cut enough of the tender inner leaves into short shreds to make 3 cups; set aside. Peel bulbs to remove tough outer skin; cut into ½-inch cubes.

In a 4-quart pan, melt butter over medium heat. Add onion and cubed kohlrabi; cook, stirring occasionally, until onion is soft (about 10 minutes). Add stock and nutmeg. Bring to a boil over high heat; reduce heat, cover, and simmer until kohlrabi is very tender when pierced (25 to 35 minutes).

Whirl half the cubed kohlrabi with some of the broth in a food processor or blender until smooth. Return to pan and add chicken and kohlrabi leaves; heat until steaming. Season to taste with salt and pepper. Makes 4 to 6 servings.

THAI FRIED EGG & PORK SOUP

Cooks in Thailand use eggs and pork together in many of their favorite dishes. In this soup, the eggs and pork are fried, then floated in a seasoned chicken broth. Accompanied by a crisp spinach salad and sesame bread sticks, it makes a noteworthy cosmopolitan meal.

> 4 eggs
> 3 tablespoons salad oil
> 1 pound lean boneless pork
> 4 cloves garlic, finely chopped
> ⅛ teaspoon pepper
> 6 cups Chinese Chicken or Pork Stock (page 5), Chicken Stock (page 5), or regular-strength canned chicken broth
> 1 teaspoon *each* sugar and vinegar
> ½ teaspoon soy sauce
> ¾ cup thinly sliced green onions (including tops)

Lightly beat eggs with a fork. Heat 1 tablespoon of the oil in a wide frying pan over medium-high heat; when oil is hot, pour in eggs and cook, gently lifting cooked portion to let uncooked egg flow underneath, until eggs are set and lightly browned; slip a wide spatula under egg and flip over. Cook other side until lightly browned. Remove from pan and cut into strips ½ inch wide and 2 inches long; set aside.

Cut pork into strips ⅛ inch thick, 1 inch wide, and 2 inches long. Combine with garlic and pepper. Heat 1 tablespoon more oil in pan over high heat. When oil is hot, add half the pork mixture and cook, stirring, until lightly browned (about 3 minutes); remove from pan and set aside. Repeat, using remaining 1 tablespoon oil and remaining pork mixture.

In a 3 to 4-quart pan, bring stock, sugar, vinegar, and soy to a boil over high heat. Add egg, pork mixture, and onions; cook just until pork is heated through (1 to 2 minutes). Makes 6 servings.

MUSHROOM-SAUSAGE SOUP

Warm and nourishing are the words that describe this sausage soup with mushrooms and barley. It's great for lunch with cheese and crackers—or even for breakfast, accompanied by orange juice, milk, and buttered whole wheat toast.

> ½ pound bulk pork sausage
> 1 large onion, chopped
> 1 large carrot, thinly sliced
> ⅓ pound mushrooms, thinly sliced
> 5 cups Beef Stock (page 5) or regular-strength canned beef broth
> ⅓ cup pearl barley
> ½ teaspoon thyme leaves

Heat a 3-quart pan over medium heat; when pan is hot, crumble sausage into it and cook, stirring occasionally, until lightly browned. Add onion, carrot, and mushrooms; cook, stirring, until onion is soft (about 10 minutes). Stir in stock, barley, and thyme. Bring to a boil over medium-high heat; reduce heat, cover, and simmer until barley is tender (about 30 minutes).

Skim and discard fat. Or let cool, then cover and refrigerate, removing solidified fat the next day. Reheat slowly until steaming. Makes 4 to 6 servings.

CREAMED BARLEY SOUP WITH PROSCIUTTO

Plump, chewy beads of pearl barley contrast with tender little peas and ribbons of prosciutto in this creamy winter soup.

To complete a satisfying supper, you can add slices of pumpernickel bread and a platter of your favorite cold cuts.

> ¼ cup butter or margarine
> ¼ cup finely chopped shallots
> 1 cup pearl barley
> 5½ cups Chicken Stock (page 5) or regular-strength canned chicken broth
> ¼ pound prosciutto or other dry-cured ham, cut into thin slivers
> ¼ teaspoon pepper
> 1 cup whipping cream
> 1 package (10 oz.) frozen tiny peas, thawed
> 1 cup (3 to 5 oz.) grated Parmesan cheese
> Ground nutmeg

In a 5 to 6-quart pan, melt butter over medium heat. Add shallots and cook until soft (3 to 5 minutes). Add barley and cook, stirring, until it turns light golden in color. Stir in stock, prosciutto, and pepper. Bring to a boil over high heat; reduce heat, cover, and simmer until barley is tender (about 30 minutes). Stir in cream and peas and heat until steaming.

Top individual servings with cheese and a sprinkle of nutmeg. Makes 6 to 8 servings.

RAVIOLI & CABBAGE SOUP

Homemade or purchased ravioli can be used in this quick soup; it simmers with vegetables and bacon to make a savory light lunch or supper.

> 5 slices bacon
> 1 small onion, chopped
> 2 cloves garlic, minced or pressed
> 1 tablespoon chopped parsley
> 8 cups Beef Stock (page 5) or regular-strength canned beef broth
> 2 cups water
> 2 cups shredded cabbage
> 1 large carrot, thinly sliced
> 1 pound fresh or frozen ravioli (about 2 dozen)
> Grated Parmesan cheese

Cut bacon into ½-inch pieces. In a 5 to 6-quart pan, cook bacon over medium heat until soft and translucent. Spoon off and discard all but 2 tablespoons of the drippings. Add onion, garlic, and parsley and cook, stirring occasionally, until onion and bacon are lightly browned.

Add stock, water, cabbage, and carrot. Bring to a boil over high heat. Separate ravioli, if connected, and add to stock. Reduce heat to medium and boil gently, uncovered, stirring occasionally, until ravioli are just tender (about 10 minutes for fresh, 12 minutes for frozen).

Pass cheese at the table to sprinkle over individual servings. Makes 4 to 6 servings.

• SAUSAGE & KALE SOUP •

Portuguese linguisa sausage helps give this soup its lively flavor; kale contributes the attractive green color. (If you like, spinach or chard can be substituted for the kale.)

> 6 cups Chicken Stock (page 5) or regular-strength canned chicken broth
> 3 large white thin-skinned potatoes, peeled and cut into ½-inch cubes
> ½ pound linguisa sausage
> 2 pounds kale, spinach, or chard
> Pepper

In a 5 to 6-quart pan, bring stock to a boil over high heat. Add potatoes; reduce heat, cover, and boil gently until very tender (about 35 minutes).

Meanwhile, in a 3-quart pan, bring 1 inch water to a boil over high heat. Add sausage. Reduce heat, cover, and simmer for 15 minutes; drain. Remove sausage casings; cut meat into ½-inch-thick slices and set aside.

Discard tough stems from kale. Rinse leaves well, then cut leaves crosswise into thin strips and add to stock mixture; cover and simmer until leaves are tender (about 10 minutes).

Whirl kale mixture, a portion at a time, in a food processor or blender until greens are coarsely chopped. Return to pan and add sausage; simmer for 10 minutes. Season to taste with pepper. Makes about 6 servings.

EGGPLANT SUPPER SOUP

This robust soup gets its character from diced eggplant, tomatoes, and macaroni. Ground beef adds protein and extra flavor, and a sprinkling of Parmesan cheese crowns each serving.

> 2 tablespoons olive oil or salad oil
> 2 tablespoons butter or margarine
> 1 medium-size onion, chopped
> ¾ pound lean ground beef
> 1 medium-size eggplant (about 1 lb.), diced
> 1 clove garlic, minced or pressed
> ½ cup chopped carrot
> ½ cup sliced celery
> 1 large can (1 lb. 12 oz.) Italian-style tomatoes
> 3½ cups Beef Stock (page 5) or regular-strength canned beef broth
> 1 teaspoon *each* salt and sugar
> ½ teaspoon *each* pepper and ground nutmeg
> ½ cup salad macaroni
> 2 tablespoons minced parsley
> Grated Parmesan cheese

Heat oil and butter in a 5-quart pan over medium heat. Add onion and cook, stirring occasionally, until soft (about 10 minutes). Crumble meat into pan and cook, stirring to break up, until browned. Spoon off and discard drippings.

Add eggplant, garlic, carrot, celery, tomatoes (break up with a spoon) and their liquid, stock, salt, sugar, pepper, and nutmeg. Bring to a boil over medium-high heat; reduce heat, cover, and simmer for 30 minutes. Add macaroni and parsley; cover and boil gently until macaroni is tender (about 10 minutes).

Pass cheese at the table to sprinkle over individual servings. Makes 6 to 8 servings.

BREADS TO SERVE WITH SOUPS

Home-baked bread is a natural accompaniment for homemade soup, whether you're pairing a light broth with crisp, pastry-like cheese twists for a first course, or serving a hearty pumpernickel with split pea soup as a main dish. Other examples of well-matched soup and bread partnerships are garlicky focaccia with minestrone, and whole wheat dinner muffins with chunky vegetable soup.

Use these recipes as a starting point, and you'll soon be creating your own delightful soup-and-bread combinations.

WHOLE WHEAT DINNER MUFFINS

- 1 cup *each* all-purpose flour and whole wheat flour
- ¼ cup wheat germ
- 1 tablespoon baking powder
- ½ teaspoon salt
- 1 egg
- ¼ cup butter or margarine, melted, or salad oil
- ¼ cup granulated sugar or firmly packed brown sugar, or 2 tablespoons honey
- 1 cup milk

In a large bowl, mix all-purpose flour, whole wheat flour, wheat germ, baking powder, and salt until blended; make a well in center.

In another bowl, lightly beat egg; stir in butter, sugar, and milk. Pour all at once into flour well and stir just until dry ingredients are evenly moistened. Spoon batter into greased 2½-inch muffin cups, filling each two-thirds full.

Bake in a 375° oven until muffins are well browned and tops spring back when touched (about 25 minutes). Makes about 1 dozen.

CHEESE TWISTS

Pictured on page 18

- ¾ cup all-purpose flour
- ½ cup shredded Cheddar cheese
- ⅛ teaspoon ground red pepper (cayenne)
- ¼ cup cold butter or margarine
- 1 egg yolk beaten with 2 tablespoons water

In a bowl, mix flour, cheese, and red pepper. With a pastry blender or 2 knives, cut butter into flour mixture until it resembles fine crumbs. Stir in egg yolk mixture. Gather dough into a ball; dust with flour, wrap and refrigerate until firm.

On a lightly floured board, roll dough out to a thickness of ¼ inch. With a floured knife, cut strips ½ inch wide and 3 to 4 inches long. Holding ends of each strip, twist in opposite directions. Place slightly apart on ungreased baking sheets. (If dough becomes too soft, refrigerate again until firm.) Bake in a 400° oven until golden (about 10 minutes). Transfer to racks and let cool. Makes about 1½ dozen.

CORNBREAD

- 1 cup *each* yellow cornmeal and all-purpose flour
- ½ teaspoon *each* baking soda and salt
- ½ cup (¼ lb.) butter or margarine
- ⅔ cup sugar
- 2 eggs
- 1 cup buttermilk

In a medium-size bowl, stir together cornmeal, flour, baking soda, and salt; set aside.

In a 3-quart pan, melt butter over medium heat. Remove from heat and stir in sugar; add eggs and beat until well blended. Stir in buttermilk. Add flour mixture and stir just until dry ingredients are evenly moistened. Pour batter into a greased 8-inch square baking pan.

Bake in a 375° oven until bread begins to pull away from sides of pan (about 30 minutes). Serve warm. Makes 6 to 8 servings.

FOCACCIA

Pictured on page 39

1 cup warm water (about 110°)
1 package active dry yeast
2 teaspoons sugar
¾ teaspoon salt
½ cup olive oil
2⅔ to 3 cups all-purpose flour
3 or 4 large cloves garlic, minced
¼ cup grated Parmesan cheese

In a large bowl, combine water, yeast, and 1 teaspoon of the sugar; stir until dissolved. Let stand until bubbly (5 to 15 minutes). Stir in remaining 1 teaspoon sugar, salt, and ¼ cup of the oil. Add 2 cups of the flour.

With a heavy spoon or heavy-duty electric mixer at medium speed, beat until batter is elastic and pulls away from sides of bowl (about 5 minutes). Stir in about ⅔ cup more flour to make a soft dough. Turn dough out onto a floured board and knead until smooth and satiny (10 to 15 minutes), adding flour as needed to prevent sticking.

Place dough in a greased bowl; turn over to grease top. Cover with plastic wrap and let rise in a warm place until doubled (about 1 hour).

Heat remaining ¼ cup oil in a small pan over low heat; add garlic and cook, stirring occasionally, until soft and yellow (about 15 minutes); do not burn. Set aside.

Punch dough down and knead briefly on a floured board to release air. Roll dough with a rolling pin, then stretch with your hands to fit bottom of a well-greased 10 by 15-inch rimmed baking sheet. Place dough in pan. With your fingers or the tip of a spoon, pierce dough at 1-inch intervals. Drizzle evenly with garlic mixture, then sprinkle with cheese. Let rise in a warm place, uncovered, until puffy (10 to 15 minutes).

Bake in a 400° oven until golden brown (15 to 18 minutes). Cut into 16 pieces and serve warm or at room temperature. Makes 16 pieces.

MOLASSES PUMPERNICKEL BREAD

2 tablespoons butter or margarine
2 cups milk
1½ teaspoons salt
½ cup dark molasses
½ cup warm water (about 110°)
2 packages active dry yeast
⅓ cup firmly packed dark brown sugar
1½ cups whole bran cereal
3 cups rye flour
About 4½ cups all-purpose flour
1 egg yolk beaten with 1 tablespoon water

In a small pan, melt butter over medium heat; stir in milk, salt, and molasses. Set aside.

In a large bowl, combine water, yeast, and sugar; stir until dissolved. Let stand until bubbly (5 to 15 minutes). Add milk mixture, bran cereal, rye flour, and 2 cups of the all-purpose flour; beat until well blended.

With a heavy spoon, stir in about 1½ cups more all-purpose flour to make a stiff dough. Turn out onto a floured board and knead until smooth and satiny (10 to 15 minutes), adding flour as needed to prevent sticking.

Place dough in a greased bowl; turn over to grease top. Cover and let rise in a warm place until doubled (about 1½ hours).

Punch dough down, divide into 2 equal portions, and knead each briefly to release air. Then shape each into a smooth ball; flatten slightly. Place each loaf on a greased baking sheet, at least 10 by 15 inches. Cover and let rise in a warm place until almost doubled (about 40 minutes).

With a razor blade or sharp floured knife, make ½-inch-deep slashes on tops of loaves, forming a tick-tack-toe design. Brush tops and sides with egg yolk mixture.

Bake in a 350° oven until bread is richly browned and sounds hollow when tapped (30 to 35 minutes). Transfer to racks and let cool. Makes 2 loaves.

MAIN-DISH
SOUPS

SUBSTANTIAL DISHES

THAT ARE MEALS

IN THEMSELVES

A main-dish soup, like any entrée, serves as the focal point of the meal. Whether the occasion is a simple family supper or a more elegant company dinner, you're sure to find just the right offering from the wide range of soups in this chapter.

The choices begin with robust vegetable and bean soups, followed by fish soups and chowders, ever-popular chicken and turkey soups, and hearty meat soups with beef, lamb, or pork.

Serve a main-dish soup in a tureen, fancy pot, or casserole dish; you'll need generous-size bowls for individual servings.

ANDALUSIAN CONDIMENT SOUP

From the south of Spain comes this make-ahead party soup, an herb-seasoned blend of tomato purée, beef stock, and sweet, slow-cooked onions.

        2   tablespoons butter or margarine
        1   tablespoon olive oil
        5   large onions, thinly sliced
        3   tablespoons all-purpose flour
        1   can (about 1 lb.) tomato purée
        8   cups Beef Stock (page 5) or regular-
            strength canned beef broth
        1   clove garlic, minced or pressed
        1   tablespoon *each* red wine vinegar,
            Worcestershire, and sugar
       ¼   teaspoon *each* oregano leaves, dry
            tarragon, and liquid hot pepper seasoning
       ½   teaspoon cumin seeds, crushed
            Salt and pepper
            Meat or Seafood (suggestions follow)
            Fresh Vegetables (suggestions follow)
            Garnishes (suggestions follow)

In a 4 to 5-quart pan, heat butter and oil over medium-low heat. Add onions and cook, stirring occasionally, until golden brown and very soft (about 45 minutes).

Blend flour into onions and cook, stirring, until bubbly. Gradually stir in tomato purée and stock. Stir in garlic, vinegar, Worcestershire, sugar, oregano, tarragon, hot pepper seasoning, and cumin seeds. Bring to a boil over high heat; reduce heat, cover, and simmer for 30 minutes. Season to taste with salt and pepper. If made ahead, let cool; cover and refrigerate until next day. Reheat until steaming.

Place meat or seafood, vegetables, and garnishes in separate bowls; pass at the table to top individual servings. Makes about 8 servings.

Meat or Seafood. Choose 2 or 3 from the following: ¼ to ⅓ pound **small cooked shrimp;** ¾ pound **cooked ham,** cut into ½-inch cubes; 10 ounces **linguisa** or kielbasa (Polish sausage), cut into thin slices and browned well; and **meatballs.** To make meatballs, combine ½ pound **lean ground beef,** 1 tablespoon chopped **green onion** (including top), ¼ teaspoon **salt,** and ⅛ teaspoon *each* **ground cumin, oregano leaves,** and **pepper.** Shape into about thirty ¾-inch balls. Arrange slightly apart on a 10 by 15-inch rimmed baking sheet and bake in a 500° oven until browned and firm (about 5 minutes).

Fresh Vegetables. Choose 3 or 4 from the following: 1 cup diced **red or green bell pepper;** 1 cup diced **cucumber;** 1 cup diced **red onion;** ½ pound **mushrooms,** sliced and sautéed in 2 tablespoons **butter or margarine;** and ½ pound **carrots,** sliced and cooked.

Garnishes. Choose 3 or 4 from the following: 3 or 4 **hard-cooked eggs,** chopped; 1 to 1½ cups **sour cream;** 1 to 2 cups (4 to 8 oz.) shredded **Cheddar cheese;** 2 **limes,** cut into wedges; 1 can (8 oz.) **garbanzos,** drained; and ½ cup chopped **parsley.**

HAM HOCK BEAN SOUP

To give this rosemary-scented soup extra body and thickness, you purée about half the cooked beans and vegetables, then return them to the soup.

        1   pound dried small white beans (about
            2½ cups)
        2   tablespoons salad oil
        2   large onions, chopped
        2   large carrots, chopped
        2   stalks celery, chopped
        2   cloves garlic, minced or pressed
       ¼   cup chopped parsley
        2   pounds meaty ham hocks, cut into 2-inch
            pieces
        1   teaspoon *each* dry rosemary, thyme leaves,
            and dry mustard
        1   bay leaf
        4   cups Chicken Stock (page 5) or regular-
            strength canned chicken broth
        6   cups water
            Salt and pepper

Sort beans to remove debris; rinse well, drain, and place in a 6 to 8-quart pan. Add enough water to cover. Bring to a boil over high heat; remove from heat, cover, and let stand for 1 hour. Drain beans and set aside; discard soaking water.

Heat oil in pan over medium heat. Add onions, carrots, celery, garlic, and parsley. Cook, stirring occasionally, until onions are soft (about 10 minutes). Add beans, ham hocks, rosemary, thyme, mustard, bay leaf, stock, and water. Bring to a boil over high heat; reduce heat, cover, and simmer until beans mash easily and meat pulls easily from bones (2 to 2½ hours). Lift out ham hocks and let cool. Remove and discard skin and bones; tear meat into bite-size pieces and set aside. Skim and discard fat from soup; remove and discard bay leaf.

Whirl about half the bean mixture in a food processor or blender until smooth; return to pan. Add ham; heat until steaming. Season to taste with salt and pepper. Makes about 6 servings.

• CHILE CORN CHOWDER •

Mild Italian sausage and bacon add a delicately smoky flavor to this creamy corn soup; green chiles and pimentos lend both color and spunk.

    3 slices bacon
    1 pound mild Italian sausages, thinly sliced
    1 large onion, chopped
    1 large white thin-skinned potato, peeled
       and diced
    1 cup water
    2 cans (about 1 lb. *each*) cream-style corn
    1 can (4 oz.) diced green chiles
    1 jar (2 oz.) sliced pimentos, drained
    2 cups half-and-half (light cream)
       Salt and pepper

In a 4 to 5-quart pan, cook bacon over medium heat until crisp. Remove from pan, drain, crumble, and set aside; then discard all but 2 tablespoons of the drippings.

Add sausages and onion to drippings in pan; cook, stirring occasionally, until onion is soft and sausage slices are browned (about 10 minutes). Stir in potato and water. Bring to a boil over high heat; reduce heat, cover, and simmer until potato is tender when pierced (about 15 minutes). Stir in corn, chiles, pimentos, and half-and-half. Heat, stirring occasionally, just until steaming (do not boil). Season to taste with salt and pepper.

Garnish individual servings with bacon. Makes 4 to 6 servings.

COLORADO BEAN & TURNIP SOUP

Satisfying soup was never simpler to make—just put all the ingredients in the pot and let them simmer away, almost unattended. Accompany the soup with warm, soft pretzels and a crisp salad.

    ½ pound dried Great Northern beans (about
       1¼ cups)
    2 tablespoons salad oil
    2 medium-size onions, chopped
    1 medium-size turnip, peeled and diced
    2 large stalks celery, cut into thin slanting
       slices
   12 cups Beef Stock (page 5) or regular-
       strength canned beef broth
    2 pounds meaty ham hocks, cut into 2-inch
       pieces
       Salt and pepper

Sort beans to remove debris; rinse well, drain, and set aside.

Heat oil in a 6 to 8-quart pan over medium heat. Add onions and cook, stirring occasionally, until soft (about 10 minutes). Add beans, turnip, celery, stock, and ham hocks. Bring to a boil over high heat; reduce heat, cover, and simmer until beans mash easily and meat pulls easily from bones (3 to 4 hours).

Lift out ham hocks and let cool. Discard skin and bones; tear meat into bite-size pieces. Skim and discard fat from soup; then return ham to pan and heat until steaming. Season to taste with salt and pepper. Makes 6 to 8 servings.

• BLACK BEAN SOUP •

What goes into this party-size soup is up to the diner. Guests start with bowls of thick, well-seasoned bean soup, then add their choice of colorful condiments.

    ½ cup olive oil
    ½ pound salt pork or bacon, diced
    ½ pound Westphalian or Black Forest ham,
       diced, or 1 pound meaty ham hocks, cut
       into 2-inch pieces
    8 large onions, chopped
    8 cloves garlic, minced or pressed
    6 large stalks celery (including leaves, if
       any), chopped
    2 pounds dried black beans (about 5 cups)
    ½ teaspoon ground red pepper (cayenne)
    4 teaspoons ground cumin
   24 cups Chicken Stock (page 5) or regular-
       strength canned chicken broth
    ¼ cup wine vinegar
    1 cup dry sherry
       Condiments (suggestions follow)

Heat oil in a 10 to 12-quart pan over medium-high heat. Add salt pork, ham, onions, garlic, and celery. Cook, stirring occasionally, until vegetables are soft and lightly browned and all the liquid has evaporated (about 40 minutes).

Sort beans to remove debris; rinse well, drain, and add to pan along with red pepper, cumin, and stock. Bring to a boil over high heat; reduce heat, cover, and simmer until beans mash easily—2½ to 3 hours. (If using ham hocks, lift out and let cool. Discard skin and bones; tear meat into bite-size pieces and return to pan.) Skim and discard fat from soup.

Whirl bean mixture, a portion at a time, in a food processor or blender until smooth. If made ahead, let cool; cover and refrigerate until next day.

Return soup to pan and heat until steaming, stirring often. Blend in vinegar and sherry.

Pass condiments at the table to add to individual servings. Makes 20 to 24 servings.

Condiments. Arrange in separate bowls 3 pounds warm **kielbasa** (Polish sausage), cut into ½-inch-thick slices; 4 to 6 cups **hot cooked rice;** 2 cups finely chopped **red onions;** 8 **hard-cooked eggs,** chopped; 4 **lemons,** cut into paper-thin slices; 1½ cups **sweet pickle relish;** and 2 cans (about 7 oz. *each*) **diced green chiles.**

GREEN BEAN & SAUSAGE SOUP

Basic to German family cooking is the *eintopf*, a one-dish meal of simmered meat and vegetables. Here's one such robust dish—a sturdy green bean and bratwurst soup from southern Germany's Mosel Valley.

- 4 **slices bacon, cut into ½-inch pieces**
- 2 **medium-size onions, chopped**
- 6 **cups Chicken Stock (page 5) or regular-strength canned chicken broth**
- 4 **medium-size thin-skinned potatoes (about 1½ lbs. *total*), peeled and cut into ½-inch cubes**
- 2 **medium-size carrots, thinly sliced**
- ¼ **cup chopped parsley**
- 1 **teaspoon dill weed**
- ½ **teaspoon marjoram leaves**
- ¼ **teaspoon white pepper**
- 1 **pound green beans, ends removed and cut into 1-inch lengths**
- 1 **pound smoked bratwurst or kielbasa (Polish sausage), thinly sliced**

In a 5 to 6-quart pan, cook bacon over medium heat until crisp. Remove from pan, drain, and set aside; discard all but 1 tablespoon of the drippings.

Add onions to drippings in pan and cook, stirring occasionally, until soft (about 10 minutes). Stir in stock, potatoes, carrots, parsley, dill weed, marjoram, and pepper. Bring to a boil over high heat; reduce heat, cover, and simmer until potatoes mash easily (about 30 minutes).

With a slotted spoon, lift out half the vegetables and transfer to a food processor or blender; whirl until smooth, then return to pan. Add green beans and bratwurst. Bring to a boil over high heat; reduce heat and simmer, uncovered, stirring occasionally, until beans are tender (about 15 minutes). Skim and discard fat from soup. Makes 6 to 8 servings.

BEEF & BEAN MINESTRONE

Pictured on front cover

In Italy, minestrone varies from season to season. This springtime version is laden with green beans, zucchini, leeks, and peas.

- 2 **pounds meaty beef shank slices, *each* about 2 inches thick**
- 1 *each* **carrot, onion, and celery stalk, cut into chunks**
- 8 **cups Beef Stock (page 5) or regular-strength canned beef broth**
- 4 **cups water**
- 2 **large tomatoes, peeled and chopped**
- 3 **medium-size thin-skinned potatoes, peeled and sliced**
- ½ **cup small shell pasta**
- 1 **pound Italian or other green beans, ends removed and cut into 1-inch lengths**
- 1 **can (about 1 lb.) red kidney beans, drained**
- 2 **medium-size zucchini, sliced**
- 2 **medium-size leeks (white parts only), sliced**
- 1½ **cups shelled green peas (about 1½ lbs. unshelled) or 1 package (10 oz.) frozen peas, thawed**
- 2 **teaspoons sugar**
- ½ **teaspoon dry basil**
   Salt and pepper
   Grated Parmesan cheese

In a 6 to 8-quart pan, combine beef shanks, carrot, onion, celery, stock, and water. Bring to a boil over high heat; reduce heat, cover, and simmer until meat pulls easily from bones (about 3 hours).

Pour stock mixture through a wire strainer; reserve stock. Discard vegetables; set shanks aside and let cool. Discard bones and fat; tear meat into bite-size pieces and set aside. Skim and discard fat from stock. Return stock to pan and add tomatoes and potatoes. Bring to a boil over high heat; reduce heat, cover, and simmer until potatoes are tender when pierced (about 10 minutes).

Whirl about 2 cups of the vegetable mixture in a food processor or blender until smooth; return to pan. Add pasta. Bring to a boil over high heat; reduce heat, cover, and simmer for 10 minutes. Add Italian beans, kidney beans, zucchini, leeks, peas, sugar, basil, and meat. Cover and simmer just until vegetables are tender when pierced (10 to 15 minutes). Season to taste with salt and pepper.

Pass cheese at the table to sprinkle over individual servings. Makes about 8 servings.

• HAM & LENTIL SOUP •

Homey lentil soup becomes company fare when you serve condiments alongside—crisp garlic toast, sour cream, mint leaves, and sunflower seeds. Make the soup with regular brown lentils, or use the new red variety called "Red Chief."

> 2 packages (12 oz. *each*) brown or red lentils (about 3½ cups *total*)
> 6 cups Chicken Stock (page 5) or regular-strength canned chicken broth
> 6 cups water
> 3 large onions, finely chopped
> 4 large carrots, finely chopped
> 1 teaspoon thyme leaves
> 3 pounds meaty ham hocks, cut into 2-inch pieces
> Garlic Rye Toast (recipe follows)
> 1 cup sour cream
> About ½ cup dry-roasted sunflower seeds
> Fresh mint leaves (optional)

Sort lentils to remove debris; rinse well and drain. In an 8 to 10-quart pan, combine lentils, stock, water, onions, carrots, thyme, and ham hocks. Bring to a boil over high heat; reduce heat, cover, and simmer, stirring occasionally, until lentils mash easily and meat pulls easily from bones (about 2 hours). Lift out ham hocks and let cool. Discard skin and bones and tear meat into bite-size pieces; reserve. (At this point, you may cover and refrigerate soup and ham separately until next day.)

Before serving, prepare Garlic Rye Toast. Skim and discard fat from soup; add ham and heat, stirring often, until steaming. Transfer soup to a large tureen. Pass rye toast, sour cream, sunflower seeds, and, if desired, mint leaves at the table to spoon over individual servings. Makes 8 to 10 servings.

Garlic Rye Toast. In a small pan, melt ½ cup (¼ lb.) **butter** or margarine; remove from heat and stir in 3 cloves **garlic,** minced or pressed. Brush 24 to 30 slices **cocktail-size rye bread** on both sides with garlic butter; arrange slightly apart on rimmed baking sheets. Bake in a 375° oven until crisp and lightly browned (about 10 minutes).

RED CABBAGE & SAUSAGE SOUP

Apples and pickled beets lend a tangy flavor and an intense wine red color to this sweet-tart soup.

> ¼ cup butter or margarine
> 1 medium-size onion, finely chopped
> 2 cloves garlic, minced or pressed
> 1 can (about 1 lb.) pickled sliced beets
> 4 cups Beef Stock (page 5) or regular-strength canned beef broth
> 1 small head red cabbage (about 1 lb.), finely shredded
> 1 pound kielbasa (Polish sausage), cut into ½-inch-thick slices
> 1 large tart apple, peeled and chopped
> Sour cream

In a 4 to 5-quart pan, melt butter over medium heat. Add onion and garlic; cook, stirring occasionally, until onion is soft and golden (about 15 minutes). Drain beet liquid into pan, reserving beets; then add stock and cabbage. Bring to a boil over high heat; reduce heat, cover, and simmer for 1¼ hours.

Cut beets into thin strips; add to cabbage mixture along with sausage and apple. Bring to a boil over high heat; reduce heat, cover, and simmer until apple is tender (about 10 minutes). Skim and discard fat from soup.

Pass sour cream at the table to spoon over individual servings. Makes about 4 servings.

BISTRO-STYLE SOYBEAN SOUP

Many cooks are discovering that soybeans not only are nutritious, but taste good, too. Their rich, nutty flavor is especially apparent in this creamy purée of soybeans and leeks. If you'd prefer a heartier meat version, stir in 2 to 3 cups of cooked chicken, beef, or pork (cut into bite-size pieces) along with the half-and-half.

> 1 cup dried soybeans
> 3 cups water
> 6 medium-size leeks
> 3 tablespoons butter or margarine
> 1 small onion, chopped
> 1 cup sliced celery
> ½ cup chopped carrot
> 1 medium-size turnip, peeled and diced
> 2 cups Root Vegetable Stock (page 6), Beef Stock (page 5), or regular-strength canned beef broth
> ⅛ teaspoon thyme leaves
> 1 cup half-and-half (light cream)
> Salt and pepper
> 3 tablespoons finely chopped watercress or parsley
> Lemon wedges

Sort soybeans to remove debris; rinse well, then place in a large bowl and add water. Cover and let stand for at least 6 hours or until next day.

Trim and discard ends and tops of leeks, leaving about 3 inches of green leaves. Discard tough outer leaves. Split leeks in half lengthwise; rinse well, then thinly slice crosswise.

In a 4 to 5-quart pan, melt butter over medium heat. Add leeks, onion, celery, and carrot. Cook, stirring occasionally, until onion is soft (about 10 minutes). Add turnip, soybeans and their soaking liquid, stock, and thyme. Bring to a boil over high heat; reduce heat, cover, and simmer until beans are tender to bite (about 3 hours).

Whirl bean mixture, a portion at a time, in a food processor or blender until smooth. Return to pan; blend in half and half. Heat until steaming, stirring occasionally; season to taste with salt and pepper.

Garnish soup with watercress. Pass lemon at the table to squeeze over individual servings. Makes 6 to 8 servings.

CHUNKY THREE-BEAN SOUP

Cooked pinto, kidney, and garbanzo beans are added to a rich stock fortified with beef or ham to make this filling soup. Accompany it with warm, soft wheat rolls.

- 6 slices bacon, diced
- 2 large onions, sliced
- 2 cloves garlic, minced or pressed
- 2 pounds meaty beef shanks or ham hocks, cut into 2-inch pieces
- 3 cups water
- 3 cups Beef Stock (page 5) or regular-strength canned beef broth
- 1 can (about 1 lb.) pinto beans, drained
- 1 can (about 1 lb.) red kidney beans, drained
- 1 can (about 1 lb.) garbanzos or black-eyed peas, drained
- 3 carrots, sliced
- ½ teaspoon *each* oregano leaves and marjoram leaves
  Salt and pepper

In a 5 to 6-quart pan, cook bacon over medium heat until crisp; remove from pan, drain, and set aside. Discard all but 2 tablespoons of the drippings. Add onions and garlic to drippings in pan; cook, stirring occasionally, until onions are soft (about 10 minutes). Add beef shanks, water, and stock. Bring to a

boil over high heat; reduce heat, cover, and simmer until meat pulls easily from bones (about 3 hours).

Lift out beef shanks and let cool. Discard bones and fat; tear meat into bite-size pieces and return to pan along with bacon, pinto beans, kidney beans, garbanzos, carrots, oregano, and marjoram. Bring to a boil over high heat; reduce heat, cover, and simmer until carrots are tender when pierced (about 20 minutes).

Skim and discard fat from soup; season to taste with salt and pepper. Makes 6 to 8 servings.

MEATBALL MINESTRONE

Light-textured beef and spinach meatballs are the flavor starter for this busy-day minestrone. Bow-shaped or corkscrew macaroni cooks right in the broth, adding body to the soup—and a touch of whimsy, too.

Spinach Meatballs (recipe follows)
- 1 tablespoon salad oil
- 1 large onion, chopped
- 7 cups Beef Stock (page 5) or regular-strength canned beef broth
- 1 can (about 1 lb.) stewed tomatoes
- 1 can (about 1 lb.) red kidney beans
- ½ teaspoon *each* oregano leaves and dry basil
- 1 cup *each* sliced carrots and sliced celery
- 1 cup bow-shaped macaroni or pasta twists

Prepare Spinach Meatballs. Heat oil in a 4 to 5-quart pan over medium heat; add meatballs and cook, turning often, until browned on all sides. Remove from pan and set aside.

Add onion to drippings in pan and cook, stirring occasionally, until onion is soft (about 10 minutes). Stir in stock, tomatoes, beans and their liquid, oregano, and basil. Bring to a boil over high heat; reduce heat, cover, and simmer for 10 more minutes. Add carrots and celery; cover and simmer for 10 more minutes.

Stir in macaroni; cover and simmer until macaroni is tender (about 10 more minutes). Skim and discard fat from soup, then add meatballs and heat until steaming. Makes about 6 servings.

Spinach Meatballs. Thaw 1 package (10 oz.) **frozen chopped spinach;** squeeze out all liquid, then combine with 1½ pounds **lean ground beef,** ⅓ cup **fine dry bread crumbs,** 1 **egg,** ½ teaspoon **salt,** and ¼ teaspoon **pepper** until well blended. Shape into 1-inch balls.

REUBEN SOUP

Aficionados of deli food are familiar with a sandwich known as a "Reuben," made with corned beef and sauerkraut on rye bread. Here's a soup whose flavors are reminiscent of the sandwich.

- 1 tablespoon butter or margarine
- 2½ pounds kielbasa (Polish sausage), cut into ½-inch-thick slices
- 4 cups Beef Stock (page 5) or regular-strength canned beef broth
- 1 cup dry white wine (or 1 more cup Beef Stock)
- 1 jar or can (about 2 lbs.) sauerkraut, rinsed and drained
- 1½ teaspoons caraway seeds
- 2 bay leaves

In a 5 to 6-quart pan, melt butter over medium-high heat. Add sausage and cook, turning, until well browned. Stir in stock, wine, sauerkraut, caraway seeds, and bay leaves. Bring to a boil over high heat; reduce heat, cover, and simmer for 5 minutes. Remove bay leaves. Makes 4 to 6 servings.

SOYBEAN MINESTRONE

A versatile and economical protein source, soybeans are also an excellent carrier for other flavors. Here, cooked beans simmer with vegetables, herbs, and wine in a meatless soup.

- 3 tablespoons olive oil or salad oil
- ½ cup brown rice
- 1 large onion, chopped
- ¼ pound mushrooms, halved
- 1 cup thickly sliced carrots
- ½ cup *each* chopped green bell pepper and chopped celery
- 1 can (1 lb. 12 oz.) whole tomatoes
- 2 cans (about 1 lb. *each*) soybeans, drained and rinsed
- 5 cups Root Vegetable Stock (page 6), Beef Stock (page 5), or regular-strength canned beef broth
- 1 teaspoon *each* dry rosemary, oregano leaves, and dry basil
- ½ teaspoon *each* thyme leaves and summer savory leaves
- ⅛ teaspoon ground red pepper (cayenne)
- 1 cup dry red wine
- 1 cup thickly sliced zucchini
- ½ cup chopped parsley
  Grated Parmesan cheese

Heat oil in a 4 to 5-quart pan over medium-high heat. Add rice, onion, and mushrooms; cook, stirring often, until onion is soft and golden (about 15 minutes).

Add carrots, bell pepper, celery, tomatoes (break up with a spoon) and their liquid, soybeans, stock, rosemary, oregano, basil, thyme, savory, red pepper, and ½ cup of the wine. Bring to a boil over high heat; reduce heat, cover, and simmer, stirring, for 40 minutes. Add zucchini; cover and simmer until tender (8 to 10 more minutes). Stir in remaining ½ cup wine and parsley. Sprinkle cheese over individual servings. Makes 6 to 8 servings.

HEARTY SPLIT PEA SOUP

Pictured on facing page

Split pea soup is always a favorite for cold-weather meals. This one makes a festive entrée for a winter party or picnic; it's flavored with ham and thyme.

- 2 pounds (4 cups) dried green split peas
  About 16 cups water
- 2 medium-size onions, chopped
- 2 cups finely chopped celery
- 1 cup finely chopped carrots
- 4 to 5 pounds meaty ham hocks, cut into 2-inch pieces
- 2 bay leaves
- 1 teaspoon thyme leaves
- ¼ cup chopped parsley
  Salt and pepper
  Condiments (suggestions follow)

Sort peas to remove debris; rinse well, then drain. In an 8 to 10-quart pan, combine peas, 16 cups water, onions, celery, carrots, ham hocks, bay leaves, thyme, and parsley. Bring to a boil over high heat; reduce heat, cover, and simmer until meat pulls easily from bones (2½ to 3 hours). Lift out ham hocks; let cool. Discard skin and bones. Tear meat into bite-size pieces; return to pan. (At this point, you may cover and refrigerate until next day.)

Skim and discard fat from soup; then heat until steaming, stirring often. Add water to thin to desired consistency. Season to taste with salt and pepper. Pass condiments at the table to add to individual servings. Makes 10 to 12 servings.

Condiments. Arrange in separate bowls about 2 cups seeded, diced **tomatoes**; 2 cups **sour cream**; 1 bunch **fresh cilantro** (coriander), chopped, or parsley sprigs; and 3 cups **Garlic Seasoned Croutons** (page 21) or purchased seasoned croutons.

ood always seems to taste better outdoors, and soups are no exception. Hearty Split Pea Soup (facing page) is a tempting picnic entrée; for extra color and flavor, you can add a selection of condiments to each bowlful.

SHRIMP & CORN CHOWDER

Cream-style corn gives body to this quick-to-fix soup; ground ginger adds a hint of spice.

- 3 tablespoons butter or margarine
- 1 medium-size onion, finely chopped
- 1 medium-size carrot, finely chopped
- ¼ cup chopped red or green bell pepper
- 2 cups Chicken Stock (page 5) or regular-strength canned chicken broth
- 1 can (about 1 lb.) Italian-style tomatoes, drained
- ¼ teaspoon ground ginger
- 1 can (about 1 lb.) cream-style corn
- 1 pound medium-size raw shrimp, shelled and deveined
  Salt and pepper

In a 3 to 4-quart pan, melt butter over medium heat. Add onion, carrot, and bell pepper; cook, stirring occasionally, until onion is soft (about 10 minutes). Add stock, tomatoes (break up with a spoon), and ginger. Bring to a boil over high heat; reduce heat, cover, and simmer for 10 minutes. Stir in corn and shrimp. Simmer, uncovered, stirring often, until shrimp turn pink (about 5 minutes). Season to taste with salt and pepper. Makes about 4 servings.

BOUILLABAISSE

Seasonings such as saffron, orange, garlic, and chiles characterize *bouillabaisse*, a well-known two-course soup from the Mediterranean coast of France. Diners sip the cooking broth as a first course, then enjoy simmered fish and potatoes as a main dish. A hot garlic sauce seasons both courses.

  Hot Sauce (recipe follows)
  Cooking Broth (recipe follows)
- 8 to 10 whole black peppercorns
  Assorted Fish (suggestions follow)
- 2 cups (8 oz.) shredded Swiss cheese
  Salt
  About 3 pounds hot cooked small thin-skinned potatoes.

Prepare Hot Sauce; cover and refrigerate.

Prepare Cooking Broth and pour into a 5 to 6-quart pan. Add peppercorns to broth; bring to a boil over high heat, then add any ¾ to 1-inch-thick fish steaks or fillets. Return to a boil; reduce heat, cover, and simmer for 3 minutes.

Atop fish in pan, arrange any ½ inch or thinner fish steaks or fillets, small whole fish, and shrimp. Bring to a boil over high heat; reduce heat, cover, and simmer until fish flakes when prodded with a fork in thickest part (about 5 minutes). Remove pan from heat.

With slotted spoon or wide spatulas, carefully lift fish from broth and arrange on a large platter; keep warm.

Bring broth to a boil over high heat; remove from heat. Sprinkle in cheese, stirring constantly until cheese is melted. Season to taste with salt. Pour into a tureen; ladle into mugs or bowls at the table.

Place hot potatoes on platter with fish. Offer Hot Sauce to season soup, fish, and potatoes. Makes 8 to 10 servings.

Hot Sauce. In a food processor or blender, whirl 1 **egg,** 3 tablespoons **wine vinegar,** ½ teaspoon **crushed red pepper,** 2 cloves **garlic,** ½ teaspoon **salt,** and 1 tablespoon **fine dry bread crumbs** until blended. With motor running, gradually pour in 1 cup **olive oil** in a thin stream; continue to whirl until sauce is thickened.

Cooking Broth. In a 5 to 6-quart pan, combine ½ cup **olive oil;** 1 large **onion,** chopped; 3 or 4 **leeks** (white parts only), chopped; ½ cup chopped **parsley;** and 4 cloves **garlic,** minced or pressed. Cook over medium-high heat, stirring often, until onion is soft and golden (10 to 15 minutes). Add ½ teaspoon **thyme leaves,** ¼ teaspoon **rubbed sage,** a dash of **ground saffron,** a ½ by 4-inch strip of **orange peel** (colored part only), 1 can (about 1 lb.) **whole tomatoes** (break up with a spoon) and their liquid, 8 cups **water,** 3 pounds **fish trimmings,** and 1 teaspoon **salt.** Bring to a boil over high heat; reduce heat, cover, and simmer for 50 minutes.

Pour through a wire strainer; reserve broth and discard residue.

Assorted Fish. Choose from the following (you'll need 4 to 5 pounds *total*): **Whole trout** or **sand dabs** (about ½ lb. *each*); ½ to 1-inch-thick steaks or fillets of **salmon, halibut, Greenland turbot,** or **rockfish;** medium-size **raw shrimp,** shelled and deveined.

CLAMS-IN-SHELL CHOWDER

Many countries have distinctive fish soups: *bouillabaisse* in France, *selyanka* in Russia. Milk-based clam chowder is a classic American seafood soup, served in dozens of variations across the country.

5 slices bacon, diced
1 large onion, chopped
4 large carrots, thinly sliced
2 stalks celery, thinly sliced
⅓ cup chopped parsley
1 clove garlic, minced or pressed
1 bottle (8 oz.) clam juice
2 cups Fish Stock (page 6), Chicken Stock (page 5), or regular-strength canned chicken broth
¾ teaspoon thyme leaves
2 large thin-skinned potatoes (about 1 lb. *total*), peeled and cut into ½-inch cubes
30 to 36 small hard-shell clams, scrubbed
4 cups milk
Salt and pepper

In a 3 to 4-quart pan, cook bacon over medium-high heat until crisp. Lift from pan; drain. Set aside. Discard all but 2 tablespoons of the drippings.

Add onion, carrots, celery, parsley, and garlic to drippings in pan and cook, stirring occasionally, until onion is soft (about 10 minutes). Add clam juice, 1 cup of the stock, thyme, and potatoes. Bring to a boil over high heat; reduce heat, cover, and simmer until potatoes are tender when pierced (about 20 minutes).

Meanwhile, in a 4 to 5-quart pan, bring remaining 1 cup stock to a boil over high heat. Add clams; cover and boil gently until clams open (5 to 10 minutes). With a slotted spoon, lift out clams and place in a large serving bowl (discard any unopened clams). Pour clam cooking liquid through a strainer into soup. Add bacon and milk. Heat until steaming (do not boil). Season to taste with salt and pepper. Ladle hot soup over clams. Makes about 4 servings.

CLEAR CLAM CHOWDER WITH RICE

If you're looking for a clam chowder that's a bit different, try this lean and savory version laced with brown rice and thinly sliced zucchini.

¼ cup butter or margarine
2 large onions, chopped
1 cup chopped parsley
6 cups Fish Stock (page 6), Chicken Stock (page 5), or regular-strength canned chicken broth
½ cup quick-cooking brown rice
40 to 60 small hard-shell clams (allow 10 per serving), scrubbed
1 pound zucchini, thinly sliced
Salt and pepper

In a 5 to 6-quart pan, melt butter over medium heat. Add onions and parsley; cook, stirring occasionally, until onions are soft (about 10 minutes). Add stock and rice. Bring to a boil over high heat; reduce heat, cover, and simmer for 10 minutes.

Add clams and zucchini. Return to a boil over high heat; reduce heat, cover, and simmer until clams open (5 to 10 minutes). Season to taste with salt and pepper; discard any unopened clams. Makes about 4 servings.

MIXED SEAFOOD CHOWDER

Scallops, fish, clams, and small shrimp simmer in a creamy broth for a rich, quick-cooking chowder.

5 slices bacon, cut into ½-inch pieces
1 large onion, chopped
⅓ cup chopped parsley
1 clove garlic, minced or pressed
1 bottle (8 oz.) clam juice
1 cup Fish Stock (page 6), Chicken Stock (page 5), or regular-strength canned chicken broth
2 large thin-skinned potatoes (about 1 lb. *total*), peeled and cut into ½-inch cubes
½ pound scallops, cut into 1-inch pieces
1 pound firm-textured white fish fillets, such as halibut, sea bass, rockfish, or sole, cut into 1-inch chunks
2 cups *each* milk and half-and-half (light cream)
1 can (10 oz.) baby clams
½ pound small cooked shrimp
Salt and pepper
Paprika
1 tablespoon butter or margarine

In a 5 to 6-quart pan, cook bacon over medium heat until crisp. Lift from pan; drain. Set aside. Discard all but 2 tablespoons of the drippings.

Add onion, parsley, and garlic to drippings in pan; cook, stirring occasionally, until onion is soft (about 10 minutes). Add clam juice, stock, and potatoes. Bring to a boil over high heat; reduce heat, cover, and simmer until potatoes are almost tender (10 to 15 minutes). Add scallops and fish; cover and simmer until fish flakes when prodded with a fork in thickest part (about 5 minutes).

Add milk, half-and-half, clams and their liquid, shrimp, and bacon. Heat, stirring occasionally, until steaming (do not boil). Season to taste with salt and pepper. Sprinkle with paprika; dot with butter. Makes 6 to 8 servings.

E ven landlubbers will like this seafood soup loaded with crab, shrimp, and clams. Legend has it that this San Francisco specialty, called Cioppino (facing page), was invented by the city's Italian fishermen.

• COASTAL OYSTER STEW •

Oyster lovers are sure to enjoy this thick soup-stew brimming with oysters.

- ¼ cup butter or margarine
- 1 large onion, chopped
- ½ cup chopped parsley
- 1 large green bell pepper, seeded and chopped
- 4 cups Fish Stock (page 6), Chicken Stock (page 5), or regular-strength canned chicken broth
- 1 cup dry white wine
- 2 large white thin-skinned potatoes (about 1 lb. *total*), peeled and diced
- 1 cup whipping cream
- 2½ to 3 cups shucked raw oysters, cut into bite-size pieces
  Salt and pepper

In a 4 to 5-quart pan, melt butter over medium heat. Add onion, parsley, and bell pepper. Cook, stirring occasionally, until onion is soft (about 10 minutes). Add stock, wine, and potatoes. Bring to a boil over high heat; reduce heat, cover, and simmer until potatoes are tender when pierced (about 15 minutes).

Stir in cream and oysters. Heat until steaming, stirring often. Season to taste with salt and pepper. Makes 4 to 6 servings.

• RED PEPPER CHOWDER •

A colorful white fish chowder? Here it is—a creamy soup full of mushrooms and red bell peppers. The slightly tart flavor comes from sour cream.

- ¼ cup butter or margarine
- 2 large onions, chopped
- ½ pound mushrooms, sliced
- 1 tablespoon lemon juice
- 2 large red bell peppers, seeded and thinly sliced
- 4 cups Fish Stock (page 6), Chicken Stock (page 5), or regular-strength canned chicken broth
- 2 large white thin-skinned potatoes (about 1 lb. *total*), peeled and thinly sliced
- 2 tablespoons *each* cornstarch and water
- 1 cup sour cream
- 1½ to 2 pounds firm-textured white fish fillets, such as lingcod, halibut, sole, or sea bass, cut into 1-inch chunks
- ½ cup chopped parsley
  Salt and pepper
  Lemon wedges

In a 4 to 5-quart pan, melt butter over medium-high heat. Add onions, mushrooms, lemon juice, and bell peppers. Cook, stirring often, until vegetables are soft (5 to 10 minutes). Add stock and potatoes. Bring to a boil over high heat; reduce heat, cover, and simmer until potatoes are tender when pierced (about 15 minutes).

Mix cornstarch and water. Add sour cream and 2 tablespoons of the soup liquid; stir until very smooth. Add to soup and bring to a boil over high heat, stirring gently. Add fish and parsley. Return soup to simmering; cover and simmer until fish flakes when prodded with a fork in thickest part (about 5 minutes). Season to taste with salt and pepper. Pass lemon wedges at the table to squeeze over individual servings. Makes 6 to 8 servings.

• CIOPPINO •

Pictured on facing page

Immigrant Italian fishermen are usually credited with inventing this robust soup. Traditional ingredients include hard-shell clams, shrimp, and Dungeness crabs simmered in a tomato-wine broth.

- ¼ cup olive oil or salad oil
- 1 large onion, chopped
- 2 cloves garlic, minced or pressed
- 1 large green bell pepper, seeded and chopped
- ⅓ cup chopped parsley
- 1 large can (about 1 lb.) tomato sauce
- 1 can (1 lb. 12 oz.) tomatoes
- 1 cup dry red or dry white wine
- 1 bay leaf
- 1 teaspoon dry basil
- ½ teaspoon oregano leaves
- 12 small hard-shell clams, scrubbed
- 1 pound medium-size raw shrimp, shelled and deveined
- 2 cooked Dungeness or other hard-shell crabs in shell (about 2 lbs. *each*), cleaned and cracked

Heat oil in a 6 to 8-quart pan over medium heat. Add onion, garlic, bell pepper, and parsley; cook, stirring occasionally, until onion is soft (about 10 minutes). Stir in tomato sauce, tomatoes (break up with a spoon) and their liquid, wine, bay leaf, basil, and oregano. Bring to a boil over high heat; reduce heat, cover, and simmer for 20 minutes.

Add clams, shrimp, and crabs; cover and simmer until clams open and shrimp turn pink (about 10 minutes). Discard any unopened clams. Makes about 6 servings.

SPANISH SEAFOOD SOUP

Crushed red pepper and coriander add spunk to this very lively tomato-base soup from Spain. Crusty bread spread with garlic butter is a perfect—and authentic—accompaniment.

      3 tablespoons olive oil
      2 medium-size onions, finely chopped
      2 cloves garlic, minced or pressed
      1 large green bell pepper, seeded and
         chopped
      1 can (10½ oz.) tomato purée
      2 bottles (8 oz. *each*) clam juice
      ¾ cup dry white or dry red wine
      4 cups Fish Stock (page 6), Chicken Stock
         (page 5), or regular-strength canned
         chicken broth
      2 bay leaves
      ½ teaspoon *each* crushed coriander seeds,
         crushed red pepper, dry basil, and thyme
         leaves
      ½ lemon, thinly sliced
      2 medium-size carrots, thinly sliced
      8 small hard-shell clams, scrubbed
      ½ to ¾ pound medium-size raw shrimp,
         shelled and deveined
     1½ pounds firm-textured white fish fillets,
         such as lingcod, sea bass, rockfish, or sole,
         cut into 1-inch chunks

Heat oil in a 5 to 6-quart pan over medium heat. Add onions, garlic, and bell pepper. Cook, stirring occasionally, until onions are soft (about 10 minutes). Stir in tomato purée, clam juice, wine, stock, bay leaves, coriander seeds, red pepper, basil, thyme, lemon slices, and carrots. Bring to a boil over high heat; reduce heat and simmer, uncovered, for 10 minutes.

Add clams; cover and simmer until clam shells begin to open (about 5 minutes). Add shrimp and fish; cover and continue simmering until shrimp turn pink and clams are fully opened (about 7 more minutes). Discard any unopened clams. Makes about 6 servings.

SALMON SELYANKA

Though Finland gained independence from Russia in 1917, Russian foods are still a specialty of many Finnish cooks. One such dish is this piquant salmon and caper *selyanka*—the name given to a number of Russian-style soups and stews combining fish or meat with vegetables.

      2 tablespoons butter or margarine
      1 medium-size onion, chopped
      2 medium-size carrots, chopped
      1 teaspoon paprika
      3 cups Fish Stock (page 6), Chicken Stock
         (page 5), or regular-strength canned
         chicken broth
      1 can (about 1 lb.) stewed tomatoes
      2 tablespoons *each* drained capers and
         sliced pimento-stuffed olives
      1 tablespoon wine vinegar
      1 teaspoon sugar
      1 can (about 1 lb.) pink salmon
         Sour cream

In a 3 to 4-quart pan, melt butter over medium heat. Add onion and carrots; cook, stirring occasionally, until onion is soft (about 10 minutes). Stir in paprika, stock, tomatoes, capers, olives, vinegar, and sugar. Bring to a boil over high heat; reduce heat and simmer, uncovered, for 5 minutes.

Drain salmon liquid into pan; remove bones and skin from salmon, break fish into chunks with a spoon, and add to pan. Simmer, uncovered, until steaming.

Pass sour cream at the table to spoon over individual servings. Makes 3 or 4 servings.

SMOKED SALMON SUPPER SOUP

The smoky, salty-sweet flavor of kippered salmon permeates this bright tomato soup. Look for the salmon in your market's refrigerated food section, alongside packaged cheeses and lunchmeats.

      2 tablespoons butter or margarine
      2 medium-size onions, chopped
      1 large green bell pepper, seeded and
         chopped
      1 clove garlic, minced or pressed
         About 10 ounces kippered salmon or cod
      2 cans (about 1 lb. *each*) stewed tomatoes
      ½ cup dry red wine
      ½ cup Fish Stock (page 6), Chicken Stock
         (page 5), or regular-strength canned
         chicken broth
      2 tablespoons minced parsley
      1 bay leaf
      ½ teaspoon thyme leaves
      1 tablespoon Worcestershire
      ¼ teaspoon liquid hot pepper seasoning
      2 tablespoons lemon juice
         Salt and pepper

In a 4 to 5-quart pan, melt butter over medium heat. Add onions, bell pepper, and garlic; cook, stirring occasionally, until onions are soft (about 10 minutes).

Break salmon into bite-size pieces, discarding dark skin and bones. Add to pan along with tomatoes, wine, stock, parsley, bay leaf, thyme, Worcestershire, and hot pepper seasoning. Bring to a boil over high heat; reduce heat, cover, and simmer for 15 minutes. Stir in lemon juice. Season to taste with salt and pepper. Makes 3 or 4 servings.

OYSTER SPINACH CHOWDER

Oysters, dry vermouth, and spinach are the assertive flavors in this easy chowder.

    3 slices bacon, diced
    1 medium-size onion, finely chopped
    2 cloves garlic, minced or pressed
    1 package (10 oz.) frozen chopped spinach
    ½ pound mushrooms, sliced
    ½ cup dry vermouth, Chicken Stock (page 5), or regular-strength canned chicken broth
    ¼ teaspoon *each* dry basil and oregano leaves
    1 jar (10 oz.) small Pacific oysters, cut into bite-size pieces (reserve liquid)
    2 cups milk
    2 tablespoons butter or margarine
       Salt and pepper

In a 4 to 5-quart pan, cook bacon over medium heat until crisp. Remove from pan, drain, and set aside. Add onion and garlic to drippings. Cook, stirring occasionally, until onion is soft (about 10 minutes).

Add spinach and mushrooms to pan. Cook over high heat until steaming; reduce heat, cover, and simmer until spinach is thawed (break up with a fork). Add vermouth, basil, oregano, oysters and their liquid, and milk. Heat soup until steaming, stirring often (do not boil). Add butter and stir until melted; season to taste with salt and pepper.

Garnish individual servings with bacon. Makes 3 or 4 servings.

SPRING HARVEST CHICKEN SOUP

Thin slices of toast, spread with herb mayonnaise, float in each bowlful of this light chicken soup.

    1 frying chicken (3 to 3½ lbs.)
    5 cups water
    5 cups Chicken Stock (page 5) or regular-strength canned chicken broth
    1 large onion, cut into chunks
    1 clove garlic, halved
       Toast Rounds (recipe follows)
       Herb Mayonnaise (recipe follows)
    ½ pound asparagus
    2 medium-size leeks
    ¼ pound green beans, ends removed
    ½ cup shelled green peas (about ½ lb. unshelled)
    ¼ pound mushrooms, sliced
       Salt and pepper

Remove chicken giblets and reserve for other uses; pull off and discard lumps of fat. Rinse chicken inside and out; pat dry.

In a 6 to 8-quart pan combine chicken, water, stock, onion, and garlic. Bring to a boil over high heat; reduce heat, cover, and simmer until meat near thighbone is no longer pink when slashed (40 to 45 minutes).

Lift out chicken and let cool. Pull meat from bones, tear into bite-size pieces, and set aside. Return bones and skin to pan, cover, and simmer for 30 minutes. Pour stock mixture through a wire strainer; discard bones, skin, and vegetables and return stock to pan. Skim and discard fat from stock.

Prepare Toast Rounds and Herb Mayonnaise; set aside. Break off and discard white fibrous ends of asparagus; cut off tips and set aside, then cut stalks into 1-inch pieces. Trim and discard ends and tops of leeks, leaving about 3 inches of green leaves. Discard tough outer leaves. Split leeks in half lengthwise; rinse well, then thinly slice crosswise. Cut beans into 1-inch pieces.

Add asparagus tips and stalks, leeks, beans, peas, and mushrooms to stock. Bring to a boil over high heat; reduce heat and simmer, uncovered, until beans turn bright green (5 to 7 minutes). Add chicken and heat until steaming. Season to taste with salt and pepper.

Just before serving, spread toast with mayonnaise; place about 4 toast slices in each soup bowl. Ladle hot soup into bowls. Makes about 8 servings.

Toast Rounds. Thinly slice 1 **baguette** (½ lb.); arrange in a single layer on rimmed baking sheets. Bake in a 350° oven until toasted (about 15 minutes).

Herb Mayonnaise. Combine 1 cup **mayonnaise;** 1 clove **garlic,** minced or pressed; and 2 teaspoons chopped **fresh herbs** such as rosemary, oregano, basil, thyme, or marjoram (or ¼ teaspoon *each* dry rosemary, dry basil, and oregano and thyme leaves.

CHICKEN ALPHABET SOUP

Pictured on facing page

Children of all ages are sure to enjoy this simply flavored soup, studded with alphabet macaroni.

- 2 tablespoons salad oil
- 1 large onion, finely chopped
- 6 cups Chicken Stock (page 5) or regular-strength canned chicken broth
- 3 cloves garlic, minced or pressed
- ½ teaspoon thyme leaves
- ¼ teaspoon pepper
- ¼ cup chopped parsley
- 3 medium-size carrots, thinly sliced
- ½ cup (about 3 oz.) alphabet or other small macaroni for soup
- 1 small zucchini, chopped
- 1 medium-size tomato, peeled, seeded, and chopped
- 3 cups diced cooked chicken

Heat oil in a 4 to 5-quart pan over medium heat. Add onion and cook, stirring occasionally, until soft (about 10 minutes). Add stock, garlic, thyme, pepper, and parsley. Bring to a boil over high heat; reduce heat, cover, and simmer for 15 minutes. Stir in carrots and macaroni; simmer, uncovered, until macaroni and carrots are tender (about 10 minutes).

Stir in zucchini, tomato, and chicken; heat until steaming. Makes about 4 servings.

CHICKEN & BARLEY SOUP

An old favorite takes on a fresh new flavor when you add anise seeds and orange segments.

- 3 tablespoons butter or margarine
- 1 large onion, thinly sliced
- 1 clove garlic, minced or pressed
- 6 cups Chicken Stock (page 5) or regular-strength canned chicken broth
- ¼ cup pearl barley
- ⅛ teaspoon anise seeds
- 3 small carrots, thinly sliced
- 2 medium-size oranges
- 2 cups shredded cooked chicken

In a 3 to 4-quart pan, melt butter over medium heat. Add onion and garlic; cook, stirring occasionally, until onion is soft (about 10 minutes). Add stock, barley, and anise seeds. Bring to a boil over high heat; reduce heat, cover, and simmer until barley is tender to bite (about 30 minutes). Add carrots; cover and simmer until carrots are tender when pierced (about 10 minutes).

Grate ¼ teaspoon peel (colored part only) from one of the oranges; set aside. Then cut off remaining peel and white membrane from oranges; cut segments free. Add orange peel, orange segments, and chicken to barley mixture. Cover and heat until steaming. Makes about 4 servings.

CHICKEN GUMBO

In the South, many cooks are renowned for their gumbos—thick soup-stews of chicken, seafood, or ham (or all three). Filé powder, made from dried sassafras leaves, and okra add body and flavor.

- 1 frying chicken (4 to 4½ lbs.), cut up
- 6 cups Chicken Stock (page 5) or regular-strength canned chicken broth
- 1 can (about 1 lb.) tomatoes
- 1 large onion, cut into ½-inch chunks
- 1 large green bell pepper, seeded and sliced
- 2 stalks celery, sliced
- 1 clove garlic, minced or pressed
- ½ cup cubed cooked ham
- 1 package (10 to 12 oz.) frozen okra, thawed
- ½ pound medium-size raw shrimp, shelled and deveined
- ½ teaspoon liquid hot pepper seasoning
- ½ pound fresh or thawed frozen crabmeat or 1 can (about 7 oz.) crabmeat
- 1 tablespoon gumbo filé

Rinse chicken and pat dry. Set breast pieces aside; place remaining chicken in a 5 to 6-quart pan and add stock. Bring to a boil over high heat; reduce heat, cover, and simmer for 20 minutes. Add breast pieces; cover and simmer until meat near thighbone is no longer pink when slashed (20 to 25 more minutes). Lift out chicken and let cool. Discard skin and bones; tear meat into bite-size pieces and set aside.

Skim and discard fat from stock. Add tomatoes (break up with a spoon) and their liquid, onion, bell pepper, celery, and garlic. Bring to a boil over high heat; reduce heat, cover, and simmer for 20 minutes. Add ham, okra, shrimp, chicken, and hot pepper seasoning; cover and simmer until shrimp turn pink (about 5 minutes).

Remove from heat and stir in crabmeat. Slowly add gumbo filé, stirring constantly, until well blended. Serve at once. Makes about 6 servings.

Kids love this soup, and it provides a wholesome and satisfying meal for
soup-sippers of any age. To see for yourself why it's a perennial favorite,
you need only make a kettleful of Chicken Alphabet Soup (facing page).

CHICKEN CONDIMENT SOUP

An array of condiments—simmered black beans, homemade salsa, and bright green cilantro butter—turn simply flavored chicken and rice soup into a colorful Mexican-style party entrée.

        Black Beans (recipe follows)
        Salsa (recipe follows)
        Cilantro Butter (recipe follows)
    1   frying chicken (3 to 3½ lbs.), cut up
    10 cups Chicken Stock (page 5) or regular-strength canned chicken broth
    2   medium-size onions, quartered
    1   cup chopped parsley
    5   tablespoons tomato paste
    ½   cup long-grain white rice
        Salt and pepper

Prepare Black Beans, Salsa, and Cilantro Butter; set aside.

Rinse chicken and pat dry. Set breast pieces aside; place remaining chicken in an 8 to 10-quart pan and add stock, onions, parsley, and tomato paste. Bring to a boil over high heat; reduce heat, cover, and simmer for 20 minutes. Add breast pieces; cover and simmer until meat near thighbone is no longer pink when slashed (20 to 25 more minutes). Lift out chicken and let cool. Discard skin and bones; tear meat into large chunks and set aside.

Pour stock through a wire strainer; discard onions and parsley. Return stock to pan and add rice. Bring to a boil over high heat; reduce heat, cover, and simmer until rice is tender—20 to 25 minutes. (At this point, you may let stock cool, then cover and refrigerate stock and chicken separately until next day.)

Skim and discard fat from stock; then add chicken and heat until steaming. Season to taste with salt and pepper. Pass beans, salsa, and cilantro-flavored butter at the table to add to individual servings. Makes about 6 servings.

Black Beans. Sort ½ pound **dried black beans** (about 1¼ cups) to remove debris; rinse well, drain, and set aside.

In a wide frying pan, cook ½ pound **bacon,** diced, over medium heat until crisp. Remove from pan, drain, and set aside. Discard all but ¼ cup of the drippings. Add 1 medium-size **onion,** chopped, and 3 tablespoons minced **fresh ginger** to drippings in pan. Cook, stirring occasionally, until onion is soft (about 10 minutes).

Stir in beans and 4 cups **Chicken Stock** (page 5) or regular-strength canned chicken broth. Bring to a boil over high heat; reduce heat, cover, and simmer until beans are tender (2 to 2½ hours), adding **water** if needed. Stir in bacon. If made ahead, let cool; then cover and refrigerate until next day. To reheat, stir over low heat until hot.

Salsa. In a bowl, stir together 2 tablespoons **salad oil** and 1 tablespoon **white wine vinegar.** Then stir in ¾ cup minced **red or green bell pepper** and ¼ cup minced **fresh or canned jalapeño peppers.** If made ahead, cover and refrigerate until next day; bring to room temperature before serving.

Cilantro Butter. In a bowl, beat together ½ cup (¼ lb.) **butter** or margarine, softened; ½ cup chopped, firmly packed **fresh cilantro** (coriander) **leaves;** and 2 cloves **garlic,** minced or pressed. If made ahead, cover and refrigerate until next day; let stand at room temperature for 30 minutes before serving.

COLOMBIAN CHICKEN & POTATO SOUP

Colombia is renowned for its flavorful varieties of potatoes, so it makes sense that this popular soup, called *ajiaco*, features two kinds—russet and thin-skinned potatoes. Offer this hearty entrée with knives and forks.

    1   frying chicken (3½ to 4 lbs.), cut up
    12   cups Chicken Stock (page 5) or regular-strength canned chicken broth
    2   large russet potatoes (about 1 lb. *total*), peeled and cut into 1-inch chunks
    2   large onions, finely chopped
    2   cloves garlic, minced or pressed
    ½   teaspoon thyme leaves
    ¾   teaspoon ground cumin
    1   pound small (1½-inch diameter) red thin-skinned potatoes
    3   large carrots, sliced
    1   bay leaf
    3   ears corn, husked and cut into 1-inch slices
         Condiments (suggestions follow)

Rinse chicken and pat dry. Set breast pieces aside; place remaining chicken in an 8 to 10-quart pan and add stock, russet potatoes, onions, garlic, thyme, and cumin. Bring to a boil over high heat; reduce heat, cover, and simmer for 20 minutes. Add chicken breast pieces, thin-skinned potatoes, carrots, and bay leaf; cover and simmer until meat near thighbone is no longer pink when slashed—20 to 25 more minutes. (At this point, you may let soup cool, then cover and refrigerate until next day.)

Skim and discard fat from soup. Bring to a boil over high heat; add corn. Reduce heat, cover, and simmer until corn is hot (about 5 minutes).

Pass condiments at the table to add to individual servings. Makes about 6 servings.

Condiments. Arrange in separate bowls 1 cup chopped **fresh cilantro** (coriander); 2 large firm-ripe **avocados,** pitted, peeled, and sliced; ½ cup thinly sliced **green onions** (including tops); ⅓ cup drained **capers;** 1 cup **whipping cream;** and 2 or 3 **limes,** cut into wedges.

CHICKEN SOUP WITH TORTILLAS

This delicate, cumin-seasoned soup is served with crisply fried tortilla strips. You can munch the strips like crackers, enjoying them alongside the soup, or crumble them into the creamy broth.

    Tortilla Strips (recipe follows)
1 **frying chicken (3½ to 4 lbs.)**
7 **cups water**
3 **small onions, cut into quarters**
3 **medium-size tomatoes, peeled and cut into wedges**
½ **teaspoon** *each* **crushed red pepper and ground cumin**
2 **cups whipping cream**
    Salt and pepper
½ **cup fresh cilantro (coriander) sprigs**

Prepare Tortilla Strips and set aside.

Remove chicken giblets and reserve for other uses; pull off and discard lumps of fat. Rinse chicken inside and out; pat dry.

In a 6 to 8-quart pan, combine chicken, water, and onions. Bring to a boil over high heat; reduce heat, cover, and simmer until meat near thighbone is no longer pink when slashed (40 to 45 minutes). Lift out chicken and let cool. Discard skin and bones; tear meat into bite-size pieces and set aside.

Boil stock over high heat, uncovered, until reduced to 4 cups. Pour through a wire strainer; reserve stock and onions and discard residue. Skim and discard fat from stock; set stock aside.

Return onions to pan along with tomatoes, red pepper, and cumin. Cook over medium heat, stirring often, until tomatoes mash easily (about 10 minutes). Add stock, cream, and chicken to pan; heat until steaming. Season to taste with salt and pepper.

Garnish with cilantro. Offer tortilla pieces alongside. Makes about 6 servings.

Tortilla Strips. Cut 8 **flour tortillas** (*each* 7 to 8 inches in diameter) into 1-inch-wide strips.

In a wide frying pan, heat ½ cup **salad oil** to 350°F on a deep-frying thermometer. Add tortilla strips, a few at a time, and cook, turning, until golden brown. Drain well on paper towels and serve warm. Or let cool, then store airtight until next day. To reheat, spread in a single layer on an ungreased baking sheet; bake in a 350° oven until heated through (about 10 minutes).

POST-HOLIDAY TURKEY CHOWDER

If there's still some meat left on the turkey after the holiday dinner is over, you have the makings for this unusual spicy-sweet soup. Use the bones to make a stock seasoned with allspice and sage—then add fresh yams, corn, and chunks of turkey.

    Turkey Stock (recipe follows)
2 **tablespoons butter or margarine**
1 **large onion, chopped**
1½ **pounds yams or sweet potatoes, peeled and cut into ½-inch cubes**
1 **package (10 oz.) frozen corn, thawed**
3 **to 4 cups diced cooked turkey**
    Salt and pepper
    Snipped chives or chopped green onions (including tops)

Prepare Turkey Stock and set aside.

In a 5 to 6-quart pan, melt butter over medium heat. Add onion and yams and cook, stirring occasionally, until onion is soft (about 10 minutes).

Add stock and bring to a boil over high heat; reduce heat, cover, and simmer until yams mash easily (about 20 minutes). Add corn and turkey and heat until steaming. Season to taste with salt and pepper; garnish individual servings with chives. Makes about 6 servings.

Turkey Stock. Pull off and dice meat from a **roasted turkey carcass;** reserve to use in soup (you'll need 3 to 4 cups meat). Break carcass into pieces to fit into a 6 to 8-quart pan. Add 1 large **onion,** cut into chunks; 2 stalks **celery,** cut into chunks; 1 teaspoon *each* **rubbed sage** and **ground allspice;** 2 teaspoons **poultry seasoning;** 8 cups **Chicken Stock** (page 5) or regular-strength canned chicken broth; and 1 cup **whipping cream.**

Bring to a boil over high heat; reduce heat, cover, and simmer for 2 hours. Pour stock through a wire strainer; discard bones and vegetables. (At this point, you may cover and refrigerate stock until next day.) Skim and discard fat from stock.

Called "soto" in its native land, Malaysian Chicken & Rice Soup (facing page)
is enhanced by condiments—bean sprouts, fried onions, meatballs,
radishes, celery leaves, chicken, rice cubes, and a chile-seasoned soy sauce.

CHILI BEEF & CORN SOUP

Not all soups require hours of simmering to develop rich flavors. This one takes just 45 minutes.

- 1 **pound lean ground beef**
- 1 **large onion, chopped**
- 1 **clove garlic, minced or pressed**
- ½ **pound mushrooms, sliced**
- 1 **tablespoon chili powder**
- ½ **teaspoon** *each* **oregano leaves and ground cumin**
- 2 **cans (about 1 lb.** *each***) red kidney beans, drained**
- 1 **can (about 1 lb.) tomato purée**
- 3 **cups Beef Stock (page 5) or regular-strength canned beef broth**
- 1 **can (12 oz.) Mexican-style corn, drained**
  Salt and pepper
- ½ **cup shredded Cheddar cheese**

Crumble beef into a 4 to 5-quart pan over medium-high heat. Add onion, garlic, and mushrooms; cook, stirring, until meat loses its pinkness. Discard fat. Add chili powder, oregano, cumin, beans, tomato purée, and stock. Bring to a boil over high heat; reduce heat, cover, and simmer for 20 minutes. Add corn; cover and simmer for 10 more minutes. Season to taste with salt and pepper. Pass cheese to sprinkle over individual servings. Makes about 4 servings.

MALAYSIAN CHICKEN & RICE SOUP

Pictured on facing page

Every Malaysian cook has a favorite version of *soto*, a spicy chicken and rice soup with condiments.

- **Rice Cubes (recipe follows)**
- **Fried Onions (recipe follows)**
- **Beef & Potato Meatballs (recipe follows)**
- **Chile-Soy Sauce (recipe follows)**
- 1 **frying chicken (3 to 3½ lbs.), cut up**
- 1 **teaspoon minced fresh ginger**
- 1 **large onion, chopped**
- 2 **teaspoons ground coriander**
- 1 **cinnamon stick (about 3 inches long)**
- 4 **cloves garlic, minced or pressed**
- 10 **cups Chicken Stock (page 5) or regular-strength canned chicken broth**
  Condiments (suggestions follow)

Prepare Rice Cubes, Fried Onions, Beef & Potato Meatballs, and Chile-Soy Sauce. Set aside.

Rinse chicken and pat dry. Set breast pieces aside; place remaining chicken in a 6 to 8-quart pan and add ginger, onion, coriander, cinnamon stick, garlic, and stock. Bring to a boil over high heat; reduce heat, cover, and simmer for 20 minutes.

Add chicken breast pieces; cover and simmer until meat near thighbone is no longer pink when slashed (20 to 25 more minutes). Lift out chicken and let cool. Discard skin and bones; cut meat into bite-size pieces and set aside.

Skim and discard fat from stock. Heat stock until steaming. Meanwhile, wrap chicken and meatballs in separate foil packets; set in a 350° oven until heated through (about 20 minutes).

Offer chicken, meatballs, rice, onions, sauce, and condiments at the table to add to individual servings. Makes about 8 servings.

Rice Cubes. In a 2-quart pan, combine 1½ cups **short-grain (pearl) rice** and 2½ cups **water.** Bring to a boil over high heat; reduce heat, cover, and simmer until water is absorbed (about 20 minutes). Turn hot rice into a 9-inch square pan; with the back of a spoon, press firmly into an even layer. Let cool. Run a knife around edge of pan; turn rice out onto a board. With a wet knife, cut into 1-inch squares. Serve at room temperature.

Fried Onions. Thinly slice 3 large **onions.** In a wide frying pan, heat ½ inch **salad oil** to 350°F on a deep-frying thermometer. Cook a third of the onions at a time, turning until golden (about 5 minutes). Lift out; drain. If made ahead, store, covered, at room temperature until next day.

Beef & Potato Meatballs. Combine 1 pound **lean ground beef;** 1 cup peeled, shredded raw **potato;** 1 **egg,** beaten; 1½ teaspoons **curry powder;** ½ teaspoon **salt;** and ¼ teaspoon **pepper;** mix until well blended. Shape into 1-inch balls. Pour **salad oil** into pan used for onions until oil reaches a depth of 1 inch; heat to 350°F on a deep-frying thermometer. Beat 1 **egg** with 2 tablespoons **water.**

Dip meatballs, a few at a time, into egg mixture; drain briefly, then lower into oil. Cook, turning, until browned on all sides (about 3 minutes). Lift out and drain. If made ahead, let cool; then cover and refrigerate until next day.

Chile-Soy Sauce. Stir together ⅓ cup **soy sauce,** 2 tablespoons **white wine vinegar,** and 1 can (4 oz.) **diced green chiles.**

Condiments. Arrange in separate bowls ½ pound **bean sprouts,** 1 cup chopped **celery leaves,** and 1 cup thinly sliced **radishes.**

GOULASH SOUP

Ever since Columbus brought red pepper plants back from the New World, Europeans have been drying and grinding the peppers into a bright red powder called "paprika." Centuries of refinements have taken the heat out of paprika, leaving a mellow spice to season this Hungarian soup.

2 tablespoons salad oil
3 pounds boneless beef chuck, cut into 1-inch cubes
2 tablespoons butter or margarine
2 large onions, chopped
1 clove garlic, minced or pressed
1 tablespoon paprika
5 cups water
1 large green bell pepper, seeded and cut into strips
1 teaspoon caraway seeds
2 large tomatoes, peeled, seeded, and chopped
1 small dried hot red chile, crushed
2 large white thin-skinned potatoes (about 1 lb. *total*), peeled and cut into eighths
Salt and pepper

Heat oil in a 5 to 6-quart pan over medium-high heat. Add beef, about a fourth at a time, and cook, turning often, until browned on all sides. Lift meat from pan and set aside. Discard pan drippings.

Melt butter in pan over medium heat. Add onions and garlic and cook, stirring occasionally, until onions are soft (about 10 minutes). Blend in paprika; then slowly stir in water until well blended. Return meat and any juices to pan along with bell pepper, caraway seeds, tomatoes, and chile. Bring to a boil over high heat; reduce heat, cover, and simmer until meat is tender when pierced—about 2 hours. (At this point, you may let cool, then cover and refrigerate until next day.)

Skim off and discard fat from soup. Bring soup to a boil over high heat; add potatoes. Reduce heat, cover, and simmer until potatoes are tender when pierced (20 to 30 minutes). Season to taste with salt and pepper. Makes about 8 servings.

ALBONDIGAS SOUP

In this Mexican-style soup, moist meatballs (*albondigas*) poach in a chile-seasoned chicken stock brimming with colorful bits of sliced carrots, spinach leaves, and cilantro. A squeeze of lime enlivens individual servings.

1½ pounds lean ground beef
¼ cup all-purpose flour
2 eggs
6 cups Chicken Stock (page 5) or regular-strength canned chicken broth
3 cans (10½ oz. *each*) condensed beef consommé
1 teaspoon oregano leaves
2 medium-size onions, chopped
1 small dried hot red chile, seeded
6 medium-size carrots, thinly sliced
¼ cup long-grain white rice
⅓ cup chopped fresh cilantro (coriander)
¾ pound spinach
2 or 3 limes, cut into wedges

In a large bowl, combine beef, flour, eggs, and ½ cup of the stock. Shape into 1½-inch balls.

Pour remaining 5½ cups stock into a 6 to 8-quart pan; add consommé, oregano, onions, and chile. Bring to a boil over high heat; reduce heat so stock simmers gently.

Add meatballs and cook, uncovered, for 5 minutes, spooning off any fat and foam. Add carrots, rice, and cilantro; simmer, uncovered, until carrots and rice are tender (about 20 minutes).

Discard spinach stems; rinse leaves well, stack, and cut crosswise into thin shreds. Add to soup and cook, uncovered, for 5 minutes. Remove and discard chile.

Pass lime at the table to squeeze over individual servings. Makes 6 to 8 servings.

SHORT RIB & VEGETABLE SOUP

Succulent short ribs simmer with a mélange of winter vegetables in this subtly spiced soup.

3 pounds lean beef short ribs
12 cups Beef Stock (page 5) or regular-strength canned beef broth
6 *each* whole cloves and whole black peppercorns
3 bay leaves
2 teaspoons thyme leaves
4 medium-size leeks
3 medium-size turnips, peeled and diced
1 large onion, chopped
1 clove garlic, minced or pressed
2 cups shredded cabbage
2 large carrots, sliced
1 can (about 1 lb.) Italian-style tomatoes
Salt

Place ribs in a 9 by 13-inch pan. Bake, uncovered, in a 450° oven until browned (about 20 minutes).

Transfer ribs and drippings to an 8 to 10-quart pan. Add stock, cloves, peppercorns, bay leaves, and thyme. Bring to a boil over high heat; reduce heat, cover, and simmer for 1½ hours.

Trim and discard ends and tops of leeks, leaving about 3 inches of green leaves. Discard tough outer leaves. Split leeks in half lengthwise; rinse well, then thinly slice crosswise.

Add leeks to rib mixture along with turnips, onion, garlic, cabbage, carrots, and tomatoes (break up with a spoon) and their liquid. Bring to a boil over high heat; reduce heat, cover, and simmer until meat and vegetables are very tender when pierced (about 30 minutes).

Lift out ribs and let cool. Discard fat and bones; tear meat into bite-size pieces and return to pan. Skim and discard fat from soup; discard cloves, peppercorns, and bay leaves, if desired. Season to taste with salt. Makes about 6 servings.

• KRAUT & RIB SOUP •

Two kinds of cabbage—shredded green cabbage and tangy sauerkraut—go into this easy-to-assemble pork and barley soup.

> 3 to 3½ pounds country-style pork ribs
> 3 tablespoons white wine vinegar
> 2 tablespoons salad oil
> 1 large onion, thinly sliced
> 1 teaspoon caraway seeds
> 2 bay leaves
> 1 jar or can (1 lb. 12 oz.) sauerkraut, rinsed and drained
> 2 cups shredded green cabbage
> 1 can (about 1 lb.) tomatoes
> ½ cup pearl barley
> 8 cups Beef Stock (page 5) or regular-strength canned beef broth

In a 6 to 8-quart pan, cook ribs, about half at a time, over medium-high heat, turning often, until well browned. Lift out and set aside.

Add vinegar to drippings in pan, scraping pan to loosen browned bits. Then add oil, onion, caraway seeds, and bay leaves. Cook, stirring occasionally, until onion is soft (about 10 minutes). Add sauerkraut, cabbage, tomatoes (break up with a spoon) and their liquid, and barley. Return ribs to pan, then add stock. Bring to a boil over high heat; reduce heat, cover, and simmer until meat pulls easily from bones (2½ to 3 hours). Skim and discard fat from soup. Makes about 6 servings.

• LAMB & BULGUR SOUP •

Nutty-tasting bulgur (quick-cooking cracked wheat) combines with lamb shanks and vegetables in a hearty soup seasoned with cumin and cinnamon. Unflavored yogurt adds tang to individual servings.

> 1 tablespoon olive oil or salad oil
> 2 lamb shanks (about 1 lb. *each*)
> 2 large onions
> 3 cups water
> 3 cups Beef Stock (page 5) or regular-strength canned beef broth
> 1 stalk celery, cut into chunks
> 1 carrot, cut into chunks
> 3 or 4 parsley sprigs
> 2 tablespoons butter or margarine
> 2 cloves garlic, minced or pressed
> 1 cup bulgur wheat
> ½ teaspoon *each* ground cumin and oregano leaves
> ¼ teaspoon ground cinnamon
> 1 package (10 oz.) frozen peas and carrots, thawed
> 1 tablespoon lemon juice
> Salt and pepper
> Chopped parsley
> Plain yogurt

Heat oil in a 6 to 8-quart pan over medium-high heat. Add lamb shanks and cook, turning often, until well browned on all sides. Quarter one of the onions; add to pan along with water, stock, celery, carrot, and parsley sprigs. Bring to a boil over high heat; reduce heat, cover, and simmer until meat pulls easily from bones (2 to 2½ hours). Lift out lamb and let cool. Discard bones and fat; tear meat into bite-size pieces and set aside. Pour stock mixture through a wire strainer; discard vegetables and reserve stock.

Chop remaining onion. In pan, melt butter over medium heat. Add onion and garlic; cook, stirring occasionally, until onion is soft (about 10 minutes). Add bulgur and cook, stirring occasionally, until bulgur begins to brown.

Skim and discard fat from stock. Add stock, cumin, oregano, and cinnamon to pan. Bring to a boil over high heat; reduce heat, cover, and simmer for 15 minutes. Add lamb and peas and carrots; cover and simmer until vegetables are tender (5 to 7 minutes).

Add lemon juice to soup; season to taste with salt and pepper. Garnish with chopped parsley. Pass yogurt at the table to spoon over individual servings. Makes about 4 servings.

PASTRY-TOPPED LAMB & SAUSAGE SOUP

Pictured on facing page

This chunky soup is crowned with a flaky, golden brown crust. Despite its impressive appearance, it's an easy make-ahead entrée for a company meal. You can make the soup a day in advance; the next day, just reheat it, pour it into an ovenproof casserole, top with a "lid" of puff pastry, and bake.

- ¼ cup salad oil
- 3 pounds boneless lamb shoulder, trimmed of excess fat and cut into 1½-inch cubes
- 1 pound kielbasa (Polish sausage), cut into ½-inch-thick slanting slices
- 2 cloves garlic, minced or pressed
- 2 large onions, coarsely chopped
- 1 bay leaf
- ¾ teaspoon thyme leaves
- 6 cups Beef Stock (page 5) or regular-strength canned beef broth
- 2 packages (10 oz. *each*) frozen artichoke hearts, thawed
- 1 package (10 oz.) frozen peas, thawed
- 1 can (about 8 oz.) baby corn, drained; or 1 package (10 oz.) frozen baby corn, thawed
  Salt and pepper
- 1 sheet (half a 17¼-oz. package) frozen puff pastry
- 1 egg

Heat oil in a 6 to 8-quart pan over medium heat. Add lamb, about a fourth at a time, and cook, turning often, until browned on all sides. Lift meat from pan and set aside. Add sausage, garlic, and onions to drippings in pan; cook, stirring occasionally, until onions are soft and sausage slices are browned (about 10 minutes).

Return lamb and any accumulated juices to pan along with bay leaf, thyme, and stock. Bring to a boil over high heat; reduce heat, cover, and simmer until lamb is very tender when pierced (1¼ to 1½ hours).

Add artichokes, peas, and corn to pan. Bring to a boil over high heat; reduce heat, cover, and simmer until vegetables are heated through (about 5 minutes). Season to taste with salt and pepper. (At this point, you may let soup cool, then cover and refrigerate until next day.)

About an hour before serving, remove puff pastry sheet from package and let stand at room temperature, uncovered, for 20 minutes. Meanwhile, skim and discard fat from soup. Reheat to boiling.

Carefully unfold pastry; on a lightly floured board, evenly roll into a sheet that's at least 1½ inches larger on all sides than a 4 to 5-quart oven-proof casserole. With a sharp knife, cut pastry into shape of casserole, leaving 1½ inches overhang on all sides. Beat egg; with a pastry brush, spread a 1-inch band of egg around edges of dough.

Transfer soup into casserole. Carefully lift pastry with both hands and place, egg side down, on casserole (don't let pastry touch hot soup). Press pastry firmly against rim and sides of casserole.

Set casserole on lowest rack in a 400° oven and bake until pastry is puffy and browned (30 to 35 minutes).

To serve, cut pastry into pie-shaped sections and place a section in each bowl. Ladle soup into bowl. Makes about 8 servings.

SOUTHWEST MENUDO

A popular offering in the Southwest and in northern Mexico, *menudo* is a thick soup-stew made with tripe and posole (dried corn). It's often served on New Year's Day.

- 3 pounds tripe, trimmed of excess fat
- 1½ to 2 pounds pigs' feet or pork neck bones
- 1½ cups dry posole or 1 large can (1 lb. 13 oz.) yellow hominy, drained
- 1 large onion, chopped
- 2 cloves garlic, minced or pressed
- 1 can (about 1 lb.) tomatoes
- 1 bay leaf
  About 1 tablespoon chili powder
- 2 teaspoons oregano leaves
- 1 can (12 oz.) beer
- 6 cups Beef Stock (page 5) or regular-strength canned beef broth
  Salt
  Fresh cilantro (coriander) leaves

Thoroughly rinse tripe, pigs' feet, and posole (do not rinse hominy). Cut tripe into 1-inch pieces.

In an 8 to 10-quart pan, combine tripe, pigs' feet, posole (if using hominy, add later—see below), onion, garlic, tomatoes (break up with a spoon) and their liquid, bay leaf, 1 tablespoon chili powder, oregano, beer, and stock. Bring to a boil over high heat; reduce heat, cover, and simmer until tripe and posole are very tender—6 to 7 hours. (At this point, you may cover and refrigerate soup until next day.)

Skim and discard fat from soup. Add hominy, if used; heat until steaming. Season to taste with salt and additional chili powder. Pass cilantro at the table to sprinkle over individual servings. Makes 8 to 10 servings.

Break open the baked-on crust of Pastry-topped Lamb & Sausage Soup (facing page) and release a heavenly aroma. The pastry conceals a chunky, hearty soup that's full of rich meat flavor.

83

MENU PLANNING WITH SOUPS

Soups, whether warm and satisfying or cool and refreshing, can fit into any course of a menu. A delicate first-course broth or bisque can heighten appetites for the entrée that follows; a robust main-course offering becomes a one-bowl family supper or a show-stopping company entrée. But no matter when they're served, soups are always convenient, because they can be prepared almost completely ahead of time.

Here we've assembled 11 menus based on the soup recipes in this book. We hope you'll use them as a guide to planning your own casual or elegant menus.

WARM-WEATHER COMPANY BRUNCH

Reminiscent of morning meals in Scandinavia, this menu begins with a sweet-tart berry soup.

Lingonberry-Blueberry Soup (page 89)
Ham and Cheese Omelets
Cinnamon Rolls
Coffee or Tea

CHILDREN'S LUNCH

Vegetable soup filled with whimsical alphabet-shaped pasta is sure to delight your youngsters on a chilly winter day.

Alphabet Vegetable Soup (page 41)
Toasted Cheese Sandwiches
Apple Slices
Milk

ELEGANT FRENCH DINNER

Dinner in France often begins with a well-balanced vegetable soup, such as this one made from bright green watercress. While guests finish the soup, you can arrange the main course on serving platters.

Watercress Soup (page 30)
Leg of Lamb
Roasted Onions and Carrots
Mint-seasoned Baby Peas
Dry Red Wine
Fresh Fruit Tart

FAMILY SUPPER

For a family meal with a new twist, use a beef chuck roast to make Hungarian goulash soup—a thick, stick-to-the-ribs meal that will satisfy even the most ravenous appetites.

Goulash Soup (page 80)
Warm Flour Tortillas
Marinated Vegetable Salad
Beer or Apple Juice
Baked Apples

HOLIDAY OPEN HOUSE

A tureen of soup that can be kept warm on a buffet table for several hours without deteriorating, such as this split pea soup, is a perfect choice for an open house.

Hearty Split Pea Soup (page 66)
Open-faced Sandwiches: Assorted Sliced Breads, Cold Cuts, Sliced Cheese, Mayonnaise, and Mustard
Crisp Raw Vegetables
Wine Punch
Holiday Cookies

BUFFET-STYLE SPANISH SOUP PARTY

Good-looking, easy to make well ahead, and fun to serve—condiment soup is perfect party fare. Guests build their own meals from the soup and an array of substantial condiments.

Andalusian Condiment Soup (page 61)
Warm Garlic Bread
Salad of Crisp Mixed Greens
Chilled White Wine or Beer
Flan or Coffee-flavored Ice Cream

SUMMER BARBECUE

While you tend the barbecue, let your guests wander around the garden and visit as they sip a cup of golden crookneck squash soup.

Creamy Crookneck Squash Soup (page 19)
Barbecued Steak or Chicken
Corn on the Cob
Watermelon Slices
Iced Tea, Iced Coffee, or Beer
Strawberry Shortcake

SCANDINAVIAN-STYLE DINNER

Following a simple dinner of poached fish and vegetables, present a sweet, spectacular meringue-topped soup for dessert.

Poached Salmon with Dill Butter
Steamed New Potatoes
Cucumber Salad
Chilled White Wine or Mineral Water
Sweet Buttermilk Soup (page 90)
Crisp Ginger Cookies

SPRING LUNCHEON

Pink-tinged shrimp soup is just right for a special lunch in spring when the air is still cool.

Shrimp Bisque (page 43)
Croissants
Marinated Asparagus Salad
Chilled White Wine or Mineral Water
Strawberries and Cream

CLAM-DIG PICNIC

Whether you dig for the clams or purchase them at an oceanside market, making chowder with them is very easy. Prepare the soup base at home, then add the clams and zucchini, and finish the cooking at the beach. Where it's permitted, you can heat the soup over a wood fire; or bring along your own portable barbecue or gas stove.

Clear Clam Chowder with Rice (page 69)
Baguettes of Bread with Butter
and Slices of Cheese
Melon Wedges
Chilled White Wine or Beer
Fruit Turnovers

LATE EVENING REPAST

For a warming but not too filling meal after an evening at the movies, a concert, or a sporting event, try leek soup topped with toast rounds and Brie. You can prepare the soup and toast early in the day, then bake the soup just before serving.

Leek Soup with Brie (page 33)
Chilled White Wine or Cider
Poundcake with Sliced Fresh Fruit

The Mexican city of Guadalajara lends its name to this hearty main-dish soup of pork, beans, carrots, and baby corn. Serve Sopa de Guadalajara (facing page) with add-on condiments and hot tortillas for a south-of-the-border feast.

• SOPA DE GUADALAJARA •

Pictured on facing page

What could be more warming on a cool winter night than this sturdy Mexican-style condiment soup brimming with pork, red beans, carrots, and baby corn? To complete the meal, offer warm corn tortillas and sangría or beer.

  1 cup dried small red beans
  2 tablespoons salad oil
  3½ to 4 pounds boneless pork butt or pork shoulder, trimmed of excess fat and cut into 1½-inch cubes
  2 medium-size onions, chopped
  2 cloves garlic, minced or pressed
  2 teaspoons chili powder
  1 teaspoon *each* oregano leaves and cumin seeds
  7 cups water
  4 cups Beef Stock (page 5) or regular-strength canned beef broth
  4 cups thinly sliced carrots
  1 can (about 8 oz.) baby corn, drained; or 1 package (10 oz.) frozen baby corn, thawed
     Salt and pepper
     Condiments (suggestions follow)

Sort beans to remove debris; rinse well, drain, and set aside.

Heat oil in a 6 to 8-quart pan over medium-high heat. Add pork, about a fourth at a time, and cook, turning often, until well browned. Lift out and set aside.

Add onions and garlic to drippings in pan and cook, stirring occasionally, until onions are soft (about 10 minutes). Return pork and any accumulated juices to pan; stir in chili powder, oregano, cumin seeds, water, stock, and beans.

Bring to a boil over high heat; reduce heat, cover, and simmer until meat and beans are very tender—1¼ to 1½ hours. (At this point, you may let soup cool, then cover and refrigerate until next day.)

Skim and discard fat from soup. Bring soup to a boil over high heat, stirring frequently; add carrots, then reduce heat, cover, and simmer until carrots are tender (10 to 15 minutes). Add corn and heat until steaming. Season to taste with salt and pepper.

Pass condiments at the table to add to individual servings. Makes 6 to 8 servings.

Condiments. Arrange in separate bowls 1½ to 2 cups **cherry tomatoes,** halved; 1 cup chopped **fresh cilantro** (coriander); 1 cup **sour cream;** ½ to ¾ cup thinly sliced **green onions** (including tops); 2 or 3 **limes,** cut into wedges; and **bottled jalapeño sauce.**

SPANISH PORK & BEAN SOUP

Fabada comes from Asturiana, in the northern part of Spain, where locally grown white beans are simmered with three succulent pork cuts—ham hocks, pork butt or shoulder, and sausages—to make this thick garlic-flavored soup. When you serve fabada, you might accompany it as the Spanish typically do with buttered cornbread, a crisp mixed green salad, and mugs of hot or cold cider.

  2 tablespoons olive oil
  1½ pounds boneless pork butt or pork shoulder, trimmed of excess fat and cut into 1-inch cubes
  2 pounds linguisa, kielbasa (Polish sausage), or garlic-flavored sausage, cut into 2-inch lengths
  3 large onions, chopped
  2 cloves garlic, minced or pressed
  7 cups water
  7 cups Beef Stock (page 5) or regular-strength canned beef broth
  3 bay leaves
     Dash of ground saffron (optional)
     About 1¼ pounds meaty ham hocks, cut into 2-inch pieces
  1 pound dried Great Northern beans (about 2½ cups)
  8 thin carrots, peeled and cut into 2-inch lengths
     Salt and pepper
  ½ cup finely chopped cilantro (coriander)

Heat oil in an 8 to 10-quart pan over medium-high heat. Add pork cubes, about half at a time, and cook, turning often, until well browned. Lift out and set aside.

Add sausages to drippings in pan; cook, stirring, until well browned. Lift out and set aside. Add onions and garlic to drippings in pan; cook, stirring to scrape up browned bits, until onions are soft (about 10 minutes). Add water, stock, bay leaves, saffron, if desired, and ham hocks. Bring to a boil over high heat; reduce heat, cover, and simmer for 1 hour.

Sort beans to remove debris; rinse well, drain, and add to soup along with pork and any accumulated juices. Cover and simmer until beans and pork are tender to bite (about 2 hours). Add carrots and sausages; cover and simmer until carrots are tender when pierced (about 20 minutes). Skim and discard fat from soup. Season to taste with salt and pepper.

Pass cilantro at the table to sprinkle over individual servings. Makes 8 to 10 servings.

SWEET & REFRESHING SOUPS

DISTINCTIVE CHOICES

FOR BREAKFAST,

BRUNCH, OR DESSERT

Fruit soups and other sweet soups are traditional favorites in the cuisines of Scandinavia, Eastern Europe, and parts of Asia. Often sweet-tart in flavor, they're exciting additions to many menus.

For dessert, a sweet soup, such as Danish-inspired Sweet Buttermilk Soup with fluffy mounds of meringue and strawberries (page 90), makes a dramatic ending. Or try Brandied Swedish Fruit Soup (page 93), tangy with apples, cherries, and dried fruit.

Our collection of sweet soups features both hot and cold ones; some are smooth and light, others thick and chunky.

• FRESH BERRY SOUP •

This vivid berry soup can be prepared from your choice of fruit—boysenberries, raspberries, loganberries, currants—or a combination of these. If fresh berries aren't in season, you can substitute frozen berries (thawed and drained), but be sure to omit the sugar called for in the recipe. This soup is delicious hot or cold; it thickens as it chills.

    1 **cup water**
    ⅔ **cup sugar**
    4 **cups boysenberries, raspberries, loganberries, or currants (or a combination)**
    1½ **tablespoons cornstarch**
    2 **tablespoons water**
    Whipping cream or unsweetened whipped cream (optional)

In a 2 to 3-quart pan, bring the 1 cup water and sugar to a boil over high heat; add berries. Return to a boil and cook for 1 minute. (For a seedless soup, press mixture through a wire strainer and discard seeds; then return to pan and reheat to boiling.)

Stir together cornstarch and the 2 tablespoons water; stir into berry mixture and cook, stirring gently and constantly, until mixture boils and thickens. Serve hot. Or let cool; cover, refrigerate until well chilled, and serve cold. If desired, pass cream at the table to spoon into individual servings. Makes 4 to 6 servings.

• SPARKLING RASPBERRY SOUP •

This elegant, ruby red berry soup gets a sprightly sparkle from the addition of champagne. You can sweeten the soup as little or as much as you like, according to your taste and the occasion. Just before serving, add a dollop of sour cream to each serving and garnish with one perfect berry.

    4 **cups raspberries, boysenberries, loganberries, or blackberries**
    About ½ cup sugar
    ½ **cup water**
    2 **tablespoons cornstarch**
    1 **cinnamon stick (2 to 3 inches long)**
    1½ **tablespoons lemon juice**
    ¼ **teaspoon ground nutmeg**
    1 **cup chilled champagne or ginger ale**
    Sour Cream Topping (recipe follows) or sour cream

Reserve 6 of the prettiest berries for garnish; place remaining berries in a 2 to 3-quart pan and coarsely mash. Add sugar (to taste) and stir in water. Spoon off a small amount of the berry juice; add cornstarch to juice and stir until well blended, then stir into berry mixture. Add cinnamon stick and cook over medium-high heat, stirring, until mixture boils and thickens. Stir in lemon juice and nutmeg.

Let cool; cover and refrigerate until well chilled. Prepare Sour Cream Topping.

To serve, remove cinnamon stick and stir in champagne. Spoon topping over individual servings and top each with a reserved berry. Makes 4 to 6 servings.

Sour Cream Topping. In a small bowl, combine 1 cup **sour cream,** ½ cup **whipping cream,** 1 teaspoon **vanilla,** and **sugar** to taste; beat until very smooth. Cover and chill for 2 to 4 hours.

• LINGONBERRY-BLUEBERRY SOUP •

Pictured on page 94

In northern Europe, there grows a tart little red berry known as a lingonberry, which, when sweetened, makes delicious fruity creations. The Swedes combine lingonberries with blueberries to make a colorful breakfast soup. Look for canned lingonberries in the fancy food section of your market.

    2 **cups water**
    3 **tablespoons quick-cooking tapioca**
    ½ **cup sugar**
    ¼ **teaspoon salt**
    2 **cinnamon sticks (*each* 1½ inches long)**
    About 1 teaspoon grated lemon peel
    ⅓ **cup lemon juice**
    1½ **cups (about 8 oz.) frozen unsweetened blueberries**
    1 **jar (14 oz.) lingonberries, packed in sugar**
    Sour cream
    Cinnamon sticks (optional)

In a 2 to 3-quart pan, combine water, tapioca, sugar, salt, the 2 cinnamon sticks, 1 teaspoon of the lemon peel, lemon juice, and blueberries. Bring to a boil over medium-high heat, stirring; reduce heat and simmer, stirring constantly, for 5 minutes. Remove from heat and stir in lingonberries until blended.

Let cool; cover and refrigerate until well chilled. Remove cinnamon sticks and serve cold. Pass sour cream at the table to spoon over individual servings. If desired, garnish with additional lemon peel and cinnamon sticks. Makes about 6 servings.

SWEET BUTTERMILK SOUP

Pictured on facing page

This Scandinavian dessert soup is made of lightly sweetened, chilled buttermilk topped with fluffy meringue and berries. For variety, try making the almond and orange versions. The almond-flavored one is especially delicious with strawberries or raspberries; try the orange variation with blueberries, blackberries, or strawberries.

        3 cups strawberries, raspberries,
          blueberries, or blackberries
          Honey or sugar for berries (optional)
        3 eggs, separated
        ½ to ¾ cup sugar
        2 teaspoons vanilla
        4 cups buttermilk
          Mint sprigs (optional)

Set aside ½ cup of the berries for garnish. (If using strawberries, slice.) Place remaining berries in a serving bowl; stir in honey, if desired. Set aside.

Place egg whites in a small bowl, yolks in a large bowl. With an electric mixer, beat egg whites until fluffy. Gradually add 3 tablespoons of the sugar and continue to beat until stiff peaks form. Set aside.

Using same beaters, beat egg yolks until light and lemon colored. Gradually add up to about 6 tablespoons of the sugar (to taste) and vanilla; beat until thick and smooth. Stir in buttermilk. Sweeten to taste with more sugar, if desired.

Pour buttermilk mixture into a serving bowl. Top with spoonfuls of meringue and reserved ½ cup berries; decorate with mint, if desired. To serve, ladle soup and some of the meringue into each bowl; pass remaining berries at the table to spoon over individual servings. Makes 6 servings.

ALMOND BUTTERMILK SOUP

Follow directions for **Sweet Buttermilk Soup,** but omit vanilla; instead, add ¼ teaspoon **almond extract.** Sprinkle ¼ cup **sliced almonds** over soup with the ½ cup berries. Serve as directed.

ORANGE BUTTERMILK SOUP

Follow directions for **Sweet Buttermilk Soup,** but omit vanilla; instead, add ¼ cup **orange-flavored liqueur** or ¼ cup thawed orange juice concentrate. Sprinkle 1 teaspoon grated **orange peel** over soup with the ½ cup berries. Serve as directed.

CRANBERRY SOUP

You start with cranberry juice cocktail to make this colorful soup, so you can serve it any time of year.

        ¾ cup sugar
        6 tablespoons cornstarch
        3 cups *each* cranberry juice cocktail
          and water
        1 cinnamon stick (2 to 3 inches long)
        2 whole cloves
          Whipped cream
          Sliced almonds

In a 2 to 3-quart pan, stir together sugar and cornstarch. Gradually blend in cranberry juice cocktail and water. Add cinnamon stick and cloves; bring to a boil over high heat, stirring constantly. Let cool; cover and refrigerate until well chilled. Remove cinnamon stick and cloves.

Garnish individual servings with whipped cream and almonds. Makes about 6 servings.

SPICED RHUBARB SOUP

Delicate pink in color, spiced rhubarb soup makes a refreshing opening to a warm-weather luncheon.

        4 cups diced rhubarb (about 1¼ lbs.)
      4½ cups water
        1 cup sugar
        1 teaspoon grated orange peel
        1 cinnamon stick (about 3 inches long)
        2 tablespoons cornstarch
        ½ teaspoon vanilla
          Red food color (optional)
          About ½ cup chilled white wine
          Thin orange slices
          Whole cloves

In a 3-quart pan, combine rhubarb, 4 cups of the water, sugar, orange peel, and cinnamon stick. Bring to a boil over medium-high heat; reduce heat, cover, and simmer for 20 minutes.

Mix cornstarch and remaining ½ cup water; stir into hot rhubarb mixture. Cook, stirring, until mixture boils and thickens. Remove from heat; stir in vanilla and a few drops of food color, if desired.

Let cool; cover and refrigerate until well chilled. Remove cinnamon stick. Ladle soup into individual bowls and stir about a tablespoon of wine into each. Garnish with orange slices studded with cloves. Makes 6 to 8 servings.

T**his intriguing Danish dessert delight,** Sweet Buttermilk Soup (facing page) combines cold sweetened buttermilk, clouds of meringue, and fresh berries. If you like, offer a plateful of Danish butter cookies alongside.

Orange Custard Soup

Dig deep into this Oriental-style chilled soup to discover its surprise—cold orange soup and succulent fruit top the bottom layer of delicate, velvety custard.

> 2 eggs
> 2 tablespoons sugar
> ⅛ teaspoon salt
> ¼ teaspoon almond extract
> 1½ cups milk, scalded
>   Boiling water
> ⅓ cup sugar
> 1 tablespoon cornstarch
> 2 cups orange juice
> 1 teaspoon grated orange peel
> 1 can (11 oz.) mandarin oranges, drained
> 1 can (about 8 oz.) lichees or pineapple tidbits, drained

Set four 1½ to 2-cup ovenproof soup bowls in a deep baking pan. In a large bowl, beat eggs, the 2 tablespoons sugar, salt, and almond extract; gradually beat in scalded milk. Pour egg mixture equally into the 4 bowls. Set baking pan with bowls in a 350° oven; pour boiling water into pan to same height as egg mixture in bowls. Bake until custard jiggles only slightly when pan is gently shaken (18 to 20 minutes). Lift out bowls and let cool; cover and refrigerate until well chilled.

Meanwhile, in a 2 to 3-quart pan, stir together the ⅓ cup sugar and cornstarch; gradually stir in orange juice. Cook over medium heat, stirring, until mixture boils and thickens. Remove from heat and stir in orange peel, mandarin oranges, and lichees. Let cool; cover and refrigerate until well chilled.

To serve, ladle orange soup over custard in each bowl. Makes 4 servings.

Citrus Consommé

From Martinique in the West Indies comes this icy cold consommé—a light, refreshing soup of pure citrus juice and fruit, thickened with gelatin.

> 2 or 3 small grapefruit or large oranges
> 1 envelope unflavored gelatin
> 2 cups orange juice
> 3 tablespoons sugar
> 3 tablespoons lemon or lime juice
>   Mint sprigs

Holding fruit over a bowl to catch juices, cut peel and white membrane from grapefruit and lift out segments (you should have about 1 cup). Set aside.

In a 2 to 3-quart pan, combine gelatin and ½ cup of the orange juice; let stand until softened (about 5 minutes), then stir over low heat until gelatin is dissolved. Add remaining 1½ cups orange juice, sugar, and lemon juice and stir until the sugar is dissolved.

Reserve 4 to 6 of the grapefruit segments; cut remaining fruit into bite-size pieces and add with any juices to gelatin mixture. Stir until blended. Cover and refrigerate until well chilled. Serve cold, stirring to break up if set (consommé should be consistency of thick soup). Garnish individual servings with reserved fruit segments and mint. Makes 4 to 6 servings.

Lemon Meringue Soup

Frothy and refreshing, lemon meringue soup tastes like lemon meringue pie, but is easier to make and has fewer calories.

> ¼ cup cornstarch
> 4 cups water
> 2 lemons
> ¾ cup sugar
> 2 egg yolks, lightly beaten
> 4 egg whites
>   Thin lemon slices

Stir together cornstarch and a small amount of the water; combine with remaining water in a 2 to 3-quart pan. Using a vegetable peeler, pare colored part of peel from lemons in long strips. Then juice lemons. Add peel and juice to cornstarch mixture along with ¼ cup of the sugar. Cook over medium-high heat, stirring, until mixture boils and thickens. Remove from heat.

Slowly pour a small amount of the hot mixture into egg yolks, stirring constantly; gradually pour yolk mixture into soup, stirring constantly. Remove peel, if desired. Let cool; cover and refrigerate until well chilled.

With an electric mixer, beat egg whites until fluffy. Gradually add remaining ½ cup sugar and continue to beat until whites hold stiff, glossy peaks. Reserve a small amount of the meringue for garnish; whip cold soup into remaining meringue. Serve immediately; top individual servings with a dollop of the reserved meringue and a lemon slice. Makes about 6 servings.

• PEACH & PLUM SOUP •

To make this cold, sweet-tart fruit soup, you first poach the fruit, then purée it. Add whipping cream, sour cream, or plain yogurt to the fruit purée; each gives a distinct character to the soup. With whipping cream and sour cream, you get a smooth, velvety soup, suitable for a sophisticated dessert. Yogurt lends a lighter finish, and the resulting soup is appropriate as a first course for a dinner party; or serve it with hot croissants for brunch, followed by omelets or a quiche.

- ¾ **pound peaches or nectarines**
- ¾ **pound Santa Rosa plums**
  Boiling water
- 1 **cup dry white wine**
- 1 **cup water**
- 1 **cinnamon stick (about 2 inches long)**
- 1½ **tablespoons lemon juice**
- ⅓ **to ½ cup granulated sugar**
- 1 **tablespoon** *each* **cornstarch and water**
- ¼ **cup orange-flavored or peach-flavored liqueur (optional)**
- 1 **cup whipping cream, sour cream, or plain yogurt**
  Powdered sugar (optional)

Immerse peaches and plums in boiling water to cover just until skins begin to blister (30 to 60 seconds). Lift out and plunge immediately into cold water to cover. Remove from water; with a knife, pull off skins and discard.

Cut fruit into chunks, discarding pits, and place in a 3 to 4-quart pan; add wine, the 1 cup water, cinnamon stick, and lemon juice. Bring to a boil over high heat; reduce heat, cover, and simmer until fruit mashes easily (about 15 minutes). Remove from heat and discard cinnamon stick.

Whirl fruit mixture, a portion at a time, in a food processor or blender until smooth. Return to pan and add granulated sugar (to taste). Stir together cornstarch and the 1 tablespoon water; add to pan. Cook over high heat, stirring, until mixture thickens (about 5 minutes). Remove from heat and let cool slightly. Skim off and discard any foam. Add liqueur, if desired, and ½ cup of the whipping cream (if using sour cream or yogurt, whip ½ cup with a wire whisk until smooth before adding to soup, then use whisk to incorporate smoothly). Cover soup and refrigerate until well chilled.

Beat remaining ½ cup whipping cream until just thick enough to mound; sweeten with powdered sugar, if desired. (Or sweeten remaining sour cream or yogurt to taste with powdered sugar.) Pass sweetened cream at the table to spoon into individual servings. Makes about 4 servings.

APRICOT SOUP

Follow directions for **Peach & Plum Soup,** but omit peaches and plums; instead, use 1½ pounds **apricots,** pitted but not peeled, and **apricot-flavored or almond-flavored liqueur** instead of orange-flavored liqueur. Increase granulated sugar to ¾ to 1 cup or to taste.

CHERRY SOUP

Follow directions for **Peach & Plum Soup,** but omit peaches and plums; instead, use 1½ pounds **Bing cherries,** pitted but not peeled, and **kirsch** instead of orange-flavored liqueur. Reduce granulated sugar to ¼ to ⅓ cup or to taste.

• BRANDIED SWEDISH FRUIT SOUP •

Dried fruits, cinnamon, and brandy make this soup a wonderful winter dessert when served hot. Or, if you prefer, you can prepare it ahead of time and refrigerate to serve cold. In either case, a dollop of whipped cream is a delicious—and festive—crowning touch.

- 2 **cups water**
- 6 **ounces pitted prunes**
- ½ **cup** *each* **golden raisins and dried apricots**
- 2 **small Golden Delicious apples (peeled, if desired), cored and cut into ¼-inch slices**
- ½ **cup sugar**
- 1 **cinnamon stick (about 3 inches long)**
- 1 **can (about 1 lb.) pitted sweet cherries**
- 4 **teaspoons cornstarch**
- ¼ **cup brandy**
  Whipped cream (optional)

In a 2 to 3-quart pan, combine water, prunes, raisins, apricots, apples, sugar, and cinnamon stick. Bring to a boil over high heat; reduce heat, cover, and simmer until apples are tender (about 5 minutes).

Add cherries, reserving juice. Stir cornstarch into juice, then stir into fruit mixture. Cook, stirring, until mixture boils and thickens (fruits should retain their shapes). Remove from heat and stir in brandy.

Serve hot. Or let cool; cover, refrigerate until well chilled, and serve cold. If desired, pass whipped cream at the table to spoon over individual servings. Makes about 6 servings.

Breakfast will beckon when the offering is Lingonberry-Blueberry Soup
(page 89), a sweet-tart treat of Swedish origin. Crowned with sour
cream and lemon peel, it seems to sparkle with deep, jewel-like color.

INDEX

METRIC CONVERSION TABLE

To Change	To	Multiply by
ounces (oz.)	grams (g)	28
pounds (lbs.)	kilograms (kg)	0.45
teaspoons	milliliters (ml)	5
tablespoons	milliliters (ml)	15
fluid ounces (fl. oz.)	milliliters (ml)	30
cups	liters (l)	0.24
pints (pt.)	liters (l)	0.47
quarts (qt.)	liters (l)	0.95
gallons (gal.)	liters (l)	3.8
Fahrenheit temperature (°F)	Celsius temperature (°C)	5/9 after subtracting 32